K2

IT//Audit//Security

www.mascotbooks.com

IT Auditing – Defined

For more information, please contact:
Mascot Books
620 Herndon Parkway #320
Herndon, VA 20170
info@mascotbooks.com

CPSIA Code: PRV0221A
Library of Congress Control Number: 2020914060
ISBN-13: 978-1-64543-514-3

Printed in the United States of America

IT AUDITING
DEFINED

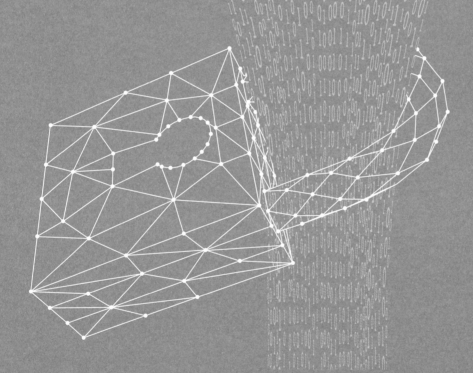

IBRAHIM YUSSUF
CISA, CISM, FITSP-A

MATTHEW ROBINETT
CISSP, CCSP, CISA, COBIT, MSIS

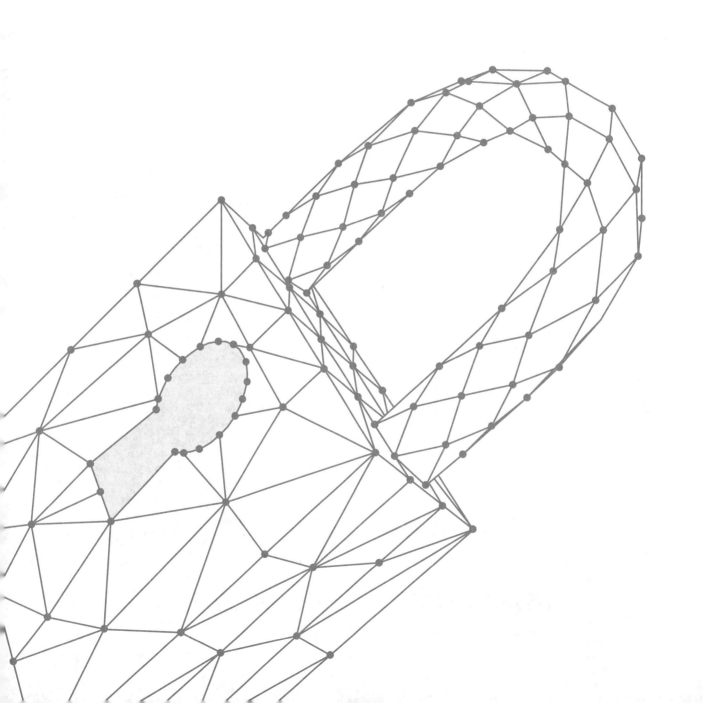

ACKNOWLEDGMENTS

● ●

First and foremost, I want to thank God (Allah), as without him, none of this would have been possible. He is my everything, my guide, and the owner of my soul.

I would also like to thank:

My Mom, Razia Abba, for always believing in me and my abilities;

My sister, Andalib Yussuf, for always helping to grow my business and doing those things which are the most difficult;

My brothers, Moayed and Sajid, for allowing me to pick their brains on technical content and ideas;

My father, for always encouraging me to push myself beyond limits; and

My son, Buggy, for being born.

Lastly, I would like to thank my Co-Author, Mathew Robinett. He saw the potential of this book and was gracious enough to join hands with me to create a masterpiece in an arena that has not been explored to its magnitude. His wealth of knowledge and experience within the IT Audit space allowed us to craft a message that will allow readers to truly grasp the meaning of Information Technology Audit.

This book is dedicated to my son, my "why," Harun "Buggy" Yussuf.

—Ibrahim

To my wife, Tyler, and my children, Owen, Lillian, and Emmett. Thank you for your love and support through the years. You help make this all possible.

—Matthew

TABLE OF CONTENTS

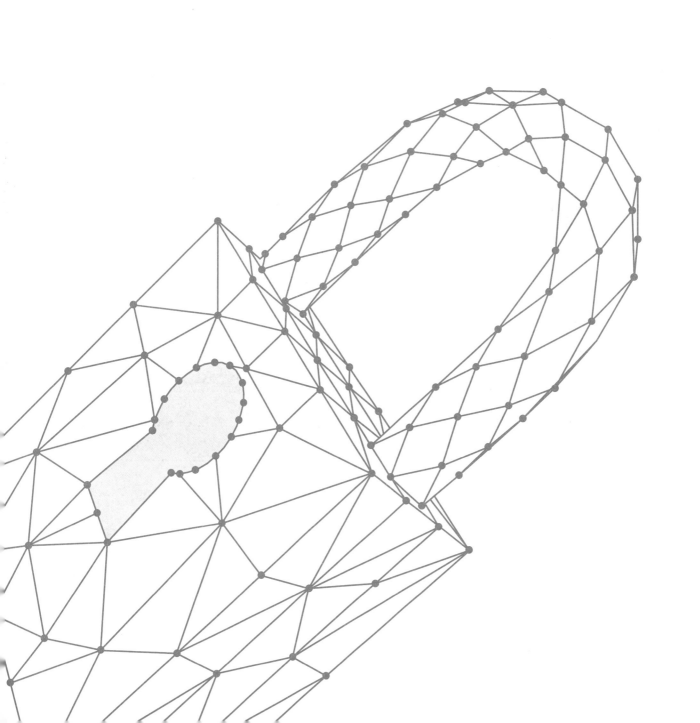

CHAPTER 1

A BRIEF HISTORY
OF AUDITING

*"Without audit, there is no control; and if there
is no control, where is the seat of power?"*

E.L. NORMANTON (1966)

• •

Auditing is a profession that has existed formally for nearly 400 years, but historical records show evidence of simplistic auditing dating as far back as the Greek, Egyptian, and Chinese civilizations. As time has gone on and the nature and complexities of business continue to evolve and expand, so has the nature of the audit function.

What once was a rudimentary system of transaction verification and fraud detection is now a critical and robust discipline that provides reliability, credibility, and accountability to an organization. For publicly traded companies, it provides necessary assurance to current and potential investors that the organization is operating in a trustworthy and efficient manner. For government and nonprofit oversight bodies, it gives assurance to taxpayers and charitable contributors that operations and management are responsible stewards of their finances.

The word "audit" comes from the Latin word *audite,* which means "to listen." What descriptors come to mind when thinking about someone listening? Silence? Focus? Mindfulness? All of these metaphorically describe the nature of the auditor's work. Essentially, an auditor is observing the organization in which they audit and documenting the current state for stakeholders, whether they be internal management, taxpayers, or shareholders.

PRIOR TO 1840: EARLY CIVILIZATION

Early records of the audit function date back to early civilizations, including Greece, Egypt, and China. The audit function primarily revolved around basic checking of business transactions. The typical market seller usually operated their business in a simple fashion—typically as the only employee or a business that was owned by one family. However, as simple businesses began to grow, they needed to hire outside help in order to continue growing their operations, and employees were required to handle money, inventory, and record subsequent transactions. As a result, theft at the hands of those employees began to significantly increase.

In order to mitigate this risk, businesses began hiring outside third parties to review their transaction records, or "books." Thus, the profession of auditing began to take shape. The primary purpose of audit in this time was to detect **fraud**.

> **Fraud:** Wrongful or criminal deception intended to result in financial or personal gain.

Fraud was detected by reviewing, line-by-line, each transaction to ensure that the record was accurate and no deception had taken place. This was possible because the recording of transactions for most businesses at this time in history was relatively minimal. As such, there was little need to develop the sampling techniques or controls testing that we see in our modern form of auditing, which will be discussed later.

1840 – 1920: THE INDUSTRIAL REVOLUTION

As the Industrial Revolution began to take hold in the United States and the rest of the world, a mass migration of people from the rural farmlands to the inner-city factories occurred. This gave rise to what we call the middle class.

A budding middle class meant that organizations would grow to become larger and more complex than ever before. In turn, businesses needed additional capital to grow faster. However, limited business and investor protection existed under United States law (there were no protective classes, like an LLC), and business owners were responsible for all debt incurred by the business. With complete liability residing with the business owner, there were many cases of owners falsifying their financial books.

While auditing techniques at this time did not change (still verifying individual transactions, line-by-line), the value that auditing provided to a business did change. Rather than only detecting fraud and error detection, audits also gave investors and business owners additional **assurance** that money, inventory, and operations of a business were being conducted in a manner consistent with the law and were managed in good faith. Investors were now able to trust business owners' financial books prior to investing, exponentially increasing business capital and further prompting growth of organizations into the larger entities we see today.

> **Assurance:** The confirmation of an organization's operations, financial statements, or other key performance indicators that give stakeholders confidence in the credibility of the examined data.

1920 – 1960: THE INVESTOR AND THE WATCHDOG

World War One had ended, and the Great Depression had devastated the United States economy. The United States' economy was slowly recovering from the associated banking crisis (with the creation of the FDIC in 1933), the virtual collapse of the stock market, and associated consumer and residential financial crises that followed.

In order to ensure that investors could continue to confidently and securely investing in businesses, expediting economic growth, and stabilizing financial markets, the United States government recognized the need to provide assurance to the potential investor that a company's financial statements were an accurate portrayal of their performance. As such, the Unites States government, still wary from the collapse of the stock market in the 1920s, created the Securities and Exchange Commission (SEC) through the **Securities and Exchange Act** of 1934.

The SEC acts as a "watchdog" to companies that are publicly traded on the various United States stock markets (NASDAQ, NYSE, BATS, and CBOE). SEC agents are federal law enforcement officers and lawyers that can prosecute and levy fines against individuals and businesses convicted of fraud or financial abuse toward investors, customers, or employees. The 1934 legislation implemented some key requirements in the marketplace for any publicly traded company that represent the backbone of the modern audit profession.

1. The Act required that publicly traded companies submit periodic performance reports on their operational and financial health. Today, this is often why you hear share values of a company rising or falling based on their "quarterly earnings report" meeting or exceeding analysts' expectations.

2. The Act created the requirements for accountants and other financial professionals in companies as they perform their core function. These requirements are called "Generally Accepted Accounting Principles" (GAAP). These requirements have established the baseline expectations for how accounting and financial professionals conduct their core duties within the United States.

The creation of the SEC helped establish a greater level of assurance for investors, which resulted in significant economic growth and laid the groundwork for our modern day audit industry. If assurance and transparency were the cornerstones of good-faith investing, how could businesses provide that?

1920 – 1960: ENTER THE AUDIT FIRM

With the implementation of the Securities and Exchange Act of 1934, the auditing profession quickly became a function that added credibility to an organization rather than just detecting fraud and error. While fraud and error detection were still major functions of the audit profession, a company established credibility when an audit firm was able to attest to the reliability of the financial data, which helped give assurance to investors. This, in turn, helped businesses obtain more investment capital.

Additionally, the complexity of businesses' operations increased dramatically from the Industrial Revolution, and the normal economic environment inherently enabled ever-growing complexity. These widespread operations and larger quantities of transactions meant that audit firms had to use **sampling** to gain a level of assurance over transaction credibility. By testing a small part of the population, auditors could extrapolate the results to the rest of the population by way of statistical confidence.

> **Sampling:** The process of selecting a certain subset of a population to make statistical inferences, thereby allowing an estimation of characteristics of the whole population.

But was sampling enough to give assurance to businesses financial statements? Suppose businesses no longer completed 100,000 transactions a year, but now completed 100,000,000 transactions per year. Sampling 10 percent of the population still meant having to examine 10,000,000 transactions. How could an audit firm reasonably test each individual transaction?

The answer? They couldn't.

In order to build credibility, auditors began to focus more on the **controls** of processes that produced the financial reports or the critical business operations, rather than only relying on individual transactional testing.

> **Control:** A policy, procedure, practice, or organizational structure that acts as a safeguard or countermeasure for managing and reducing risk to the organization. A control provides reasonable assurance that business objectives will be achieved and undesired events will be prevented or detected and corrected.

The maturation of controls testing established the modern audit profession as we know it today. If you've already had any experience with the audit profession or spent any time exposed to it, you'll notice that modern audit techniques combine several of the perspectives that have been discussed: fraud detection, error detection, assurance, financial report reviews, etc. But they all hang on the principal method of testing controls and control structures.

1960 – 1980: RISK-BASED AND IT AUDIT

As auditors matured their control testing, the profession began to understand that, as businesses grew in size, scope, and complexity, it was not possible to audit the ever-growing organizational structures, their controls, and the vast financial reporting of operations. Limited budgets for audit engagements meant a limited scope of work that could be performed. Auditors also began to understand that more value could be derived from surgical, specialized control testing. How could an audit firm deliver the most value possible with a limited budget and/or time available?

For example, would a large, regional hospital achieve a greater level of assurance and credibility by having their core mission-critical systems (patient records, medical equipment inventory, surgery scheduling, etc.) audited, or a small, peripheral marketing system? While both could present *some* degree of risk if the systems' respective data is stolen or exfiltrated, the mission-critical systems are far more important, and data loss or a breach could result in significantly more harm to the hospital. Auditing the riskiest portions of the organization's control environment meant more value, with less time devoted to auditing—hence, the risk-based audit perspective. We will cover risk-based auditing later in this book.

It was also during this time period that computers began to become a normal part of business operations. Like the previous time period, transaction occurrence became more and more voluminous. However, the complexity of transactions also increased and reliance upon automated, computer-based transactional processing increased as well. Thus, the rise of what we now call "IT auditing" began.

Auditors moved from "testing the books" to "relying on the system." Ideally, if transactions were automatically calculated and stored within a computer system with limited human interaction, wouldn't testing the controls of the system (rather than testing individual transactions) provide the assurance necessary to give more credibility to a business's operations?

1980 – PRESENT: "ADVISING" AND SOX

Throughout the 1980s and 1990s, auditing (and IT audit, specifically) largely focused on computer systems and the data they contained and reported. Control testing was now (and still is) the standard method of auditing an organization. Security fundamentals, such as confidentiality, integrity, and availability (concepts discussed in Chapter 2) all became relevant terms when planning, executing, and reporting an audit.

This time period also saw the development of "advising services." These services were the other half of the controls/compliance coin. If a business had a collection of audit findings as the result of their audit, how could they fix them? This business problem was solved primarily through consulting firms and their various services.

For example, a large consulting firm may offer both auditing and advising services. The auditing arm may produce recommendations through audit findings, while the advising arm may offer consulting services to assist in remediating these audit findings.

The auditing profession has now become a core function of the marketplace used to provide reliability and credibility to organizations. But what about accountability? Perhaps the greatest example of accountability (or failure) was the Enron scandal of 2000–2001. Using a practice called "mark-to-market" accounting, Enron used speculative values on potential trades and deals to report profits that had not been realized. Enron also hid billions of dollars in liabilities in special-purpose entities (SPEs), which created the illusion of higher profits than existed. But, based on what we've discussed about auditing and the SEC requirements, wouldn't an audit expose these types of malicious and deceptive practices?

One would think that Enron's auditing firm of choice, Arthur Anderson, would have caught these practices. However, Arthur Anderson struggled with the same tension that exists with an independent and objective auditor, with the inherent goal of generating as much profit as possible from their clients. This resulted in Arthur Anderson losing their objectivity and failing to perform due diligence and due care in the audit process.

Ultimately, Enron's deceptive and fraudulent accounting practices were uncovered, and the company went bankrupt. Arthur Anderson, by proxy, was also embroiled in controversy due to their handling of their Enron account. Enron's share value went from $90 to $1 in a matter of months, Arthur Anderson was forced to relinquish their CPA license, and both companies were eventually dissolved. Thousands of Enron employees who had their 401(k) plans attached to Enron stock values lost their entire retirement savings. Many Enron executives went to prison.

Sarbanes-Oxley Act

In response to the Enron scandal, the United States government passed the Public Company Accounting Reform and Investor Protection Act, also known as the **Sarbanes-Oxley Act** of 2002. Throughout the audit industry, it is normally referred to as "SOX."

Sarbanes-Oxley (SOX): The term used to refer to the sweeping 2002 legislation and the compliance requirements that followed, revolutionizing and enhancing the relationship between organizations needing or requiring financial credibility and the auditing firms that provided assurance to stakeholders.

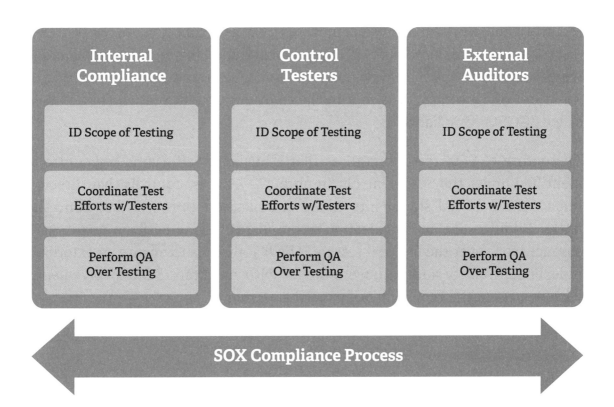

SOX established new requirements for publicly traded companies and how financial reporting and auditing were conducted within those companies. These requirements were broad and far-reaching and included key concepts such as the rules for auditor independence, accountability of principal officers (like the CFO and CEO), and increased sentencing for white-collar crimes associated with business/financial fraud. Additionally, accounting firms were now required to undergo restructuring of organizational ties to avoid potential conflict-of-interest situations, like the one Arthur Anderson involved themselves in.

Auditing SOX Compliance

With the implementation of SOX and the mandate it created for most businesses that exist in the United States economy, SOX compliance has become a main driver of audit work performed in the audit profession. While the traditional scope of audit work typically encompasses SOX as a subset of the work, SOX testing is now a required portion of a publicly traded business's annual audit work—so significant that even nonprofit and government agencies undergo some sort of rigorous SOX-style compliance testing and attestation (sometimes called "COSO compliance").

The nature of SOX testing requires that a business self-assess key controls identified under the SOX controls "umbrella"—that is, controls that directly impact the financial statements of the organization (more on key controls later). Additionally, an organization's compliance teams perform quality assurance work over the internal testing. The last piece is to ensure an external, independent entity audits those systems with no direct SOX involvement, with respect to the reporting of financial statements.

In the previous diagram, we see that internal compliance teams (not internal auditors) will identify the scope of SOX systems and their respective applications, databases, and infrastructure. Additionally, they coordinate efforts with the actual control testers to perform the testing of those controls. Often, larger organizations perform the scope development independent of external auditors.

RECAP OF KEY THEMES

Before 1840: Rudimentary process of checking transactions for fraud	**1840–1920:** First "real" audits (still transactional) used to protect investors and provide reliability	**1920–1960:** Greater investor activity and a need to add credibility to companies	**1920–1960:** Creation of SEC, GAAP, growing provision of credibility
After 1990s: SOX requires attention, controls become increasingly automated	**1990s:** Enron scandal, SOX legislation adds accountability for audit firms	**1990s:** Consulting boom takes off beyond traditional audit activities	**1960–1990:** Moving from "verifying the books" to "relying on the system," rise of advisory services

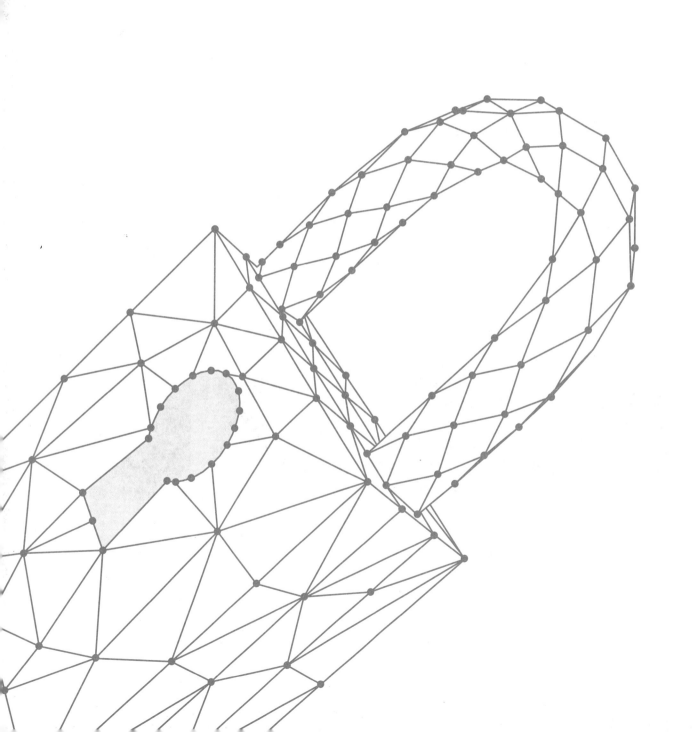

CHAPTER 2
THE BASICS OF IT AUDITING

IT auditing is a unique specialization. To be successful and competent, one must have a passion for technology and data, a passion for writing, a passion for solving real-world business problems, and a passion for people and relationships.

We can look at an **IT audit** as a method of reviewing IT controls through the lens of an independent third party (a third party that can be either internal or external).

> **IT audit:** An independent function that performs specialized reviews and assessments over the IT controls of an organization's IT environment.

From both an external and internal audit perspective, an IT auditor often represents a portion of the overall audit engagement in which the chief goal is to attest to the financial statements. We will discuss the relationship between financial and IT auditing later in this chapter. For internal engagements, there may even be complete, dedicated IT auditing teams that focus primarily on IT infrastructure.

IT auditors assess the IT controls of an IT system through evaluating the **control design** and **operating effectiveness** of the IT environment.

> **Control design:** The practice of designing controls within a business process and/or organizational environment that effectively accomplish a control's purpose, with respect to minimizing risk and enabling an organization to achieve its business objectives.

From a testing perspective, design involves inquiry with management and process owners to gain an understanding of the control environment as well as the inspection of policy and procedural documentation to verify that process owners are performing duties in accordance with policies.

As an example, when testing configuration management, a design phase would involve inquiring with the configuration management team to understand how changes are made to the system in scope, as well as reviewing the configuration management plan to determine if it contains all the necessary elements as required by National Institute of Standards and Technology (NIST) criteria and is consistent with information obtained during the inquiry or walkthrough.

> **Operational effectiveness:** The practice of maximizing operational inputs while reducing the rate of occurrence of operational errors or defects in business processes.

From a testing perspective, operating effectiveness involves obtaining a population of changes. For example, when testing configuration management and selecting a sample of changes, requesting supporting documentation to verify that changes are appropriately being requested, authorized, and tested prior to being deployed into the production environment.

It is important to note that *proper control design will lead to operational effectiveness*. Often, the auditor's work on evaluating control design will directly impact their overall assessment (audit fieldwork) and opinion on the state of assurance of financial statements. When a lack of operational effectiveness is identified in the audit, it almost always traces back to poor control design.

To better prepare an IT auditor, let us examine some core information technology concepts.

HARDWARE

Hardware makes up the physical components of the IT environment and allows all associated software and networking concepts to operate within the hardware's physical components. Hardware serves a variety of purposes in the IT environment, including processing, networking, and power management.

> **Hardware:** The physical components of the IT environment that allow applications, middleware, other associated software, and networking components to operate.

Common Hardware Components (not exhaustive):

Servers	Networking cables	Routers, firewalls, switches
Mainframes	Network appliances	Intrusion detection/ prevention sensors

Hardware devices—such as monitors, mice, and network cables—are all considered to be very low-risk to the organization. Why? Because their computing and connection nature are virtualized and do not provide effective means of an attacker or malicious insider from exploiting IT systems.

For critical hardware (such as servers, mainframes, and network appliances), these devices can be compromised and manipulated by attackers and malicious insiders into allowing unauthorized access to data and systems. This hardware is most vulnerable when it can be physically accessed by unauthorized or malicious actors who may perform actions that may disrupt operational integrity. Because software runs on hardware, incidents involving hardware issues often result in the disruption of software running on the associated hardware.

As such, hardware access must always be protected, and control testing of hardware usually focuses on this concept. Additionally, IT auditors will also focus on contingency and disaster recovery operations testing to ensure a business is able to effectively respond to a natural disaster, hardware failure, nation-state cyberattack, etc.

SOFTWARE

Software represents the logical and virtual components of the IT environment and contains the instruction sets that perform the actions and processes that allow the business to automate and calculate the system transactions necessary to perform critical functions. Software can replicate the functions of many pieces of hardware, as well as represent what we traditionally envision as software, including operations systems, applications, and middleware.

> **Software:** Programs and other operating instruction sets that allow a computer to operate, performing business processes and procedures within the IT environment.

Common Software Components (not exhaustive):

Operating systems	Basic Input/ Output System (BIOS)	Virtual servers
Applications	Drivers & utilities	Virtual routers/ firewalls

The majority of control test work performed in the audit function comprises testing on some piece of software, be it the underlying programming and coding of the software or the processes the software executes.

SECURITY

For an IT auditor to excel at their profession, it is important for the auditor to have a broad, conceptual understanding of core IT security concepts. IT audit, because of its focus primarily on security, is driven by a concept known as the **CIA Cyber Triad**, which provides the metaphorical backbone of information security.

CIA Cyber Triad: The core information security concept that places emphasis on assessing and securing data and associated IT systems along the principles of confidentiality, integrity, and availability.

Confidentiality can be considered synonymous with "privacy." Confidentialiy drives the perspective of the *principle of least privilege*, which is the idea that users within a system should only have access to the data necessary for performing their job functions. For example, in an educational enterprise system, a professor can view all grades within his or her class but cannot view the grades of the other classes their students take. Likewise, a student can view personal grades of all the classes they've registered for in this system but cannot see the grades of their fellow students. The access is based purely on a need-to-know basis to help enforce confidentiality.

Common ways to enforce confidentiality are data encryption, Public Key Infrastructure (PKI), role-based access controls, and segregation of duties, more of which will be discussed in later chapters.

Data breaches that often make the news are not cases in which data has been corrupted; rather, most breaches are an issue because of confidentiality. Large financial institutions, government agencies, and hospitals remain the greatest targets of malicious hackers, due to the value of their highly sensitive data. As such, confidentiality is typically the main driver of control development and implementation.

Integrity can be considered synonymous with trustworthiness. Integrity presents a difficult concept to protect, as most systems and business processes simply "calculate" the information given to them through repositories, such as relational databases. An attacker who can gain editable access to data most certainly violates confidentiality, but editable access also allows them to manipulate the data. For example, suppose a disgruntled database administrator (DBA) is retiring or being downsized. He may decide to change his salary in an administrative salary table in a database that he administers. The payroll process, largely automated, will process his paycheck and taxes accordingly, with no red flags going up.

To ensure proper integrity of data, we can implement various control concepts, such as the previously discussed least privilege principle around DBA access, accountability through logs reviews of DBA activity, and set up triggers that require additional approval when a salary is raised over a certain threshold. Additionally, we can implement technical solutions, such as encryption for data-at-rest, input/output data handling of web applications, and parity checks for application processes.

Breaches that affect data integrity often require effective integrity checks, extensive backup and restoration activities, as well as significant forensic analysis. The complexities and costs of these activities can be very expensive and can significantly harm the operating environment of a business.

Availability is the concept of making data available for access whenever a legitimate business need exists. Like the stereotypical IT helpdesk, staff and customers rarely care about availability until something is, well, unavailable.

Imagine waiting for tickets to the latest concert or summer blockbuster to go on sale through a ticketing website (like StubHub or Ticketmaster). You've been sitting at your computer, constantly hitting "refresh" on the webpage, waiting for the site to go live. However, the moment it goes live, the site crashes, and you're unable to buy tickets.

Has data been exfiltrated or viewed by users who shouldn't? No.

Has data been corrupted, and can the system no longer process the correct data? No.

While availability doesn't necessarily affect the quality of data or inappropriately disclosing it to unauthorized individuals, it can still significantly disrupt business operations. While the previous example impacted the ability of someone to buy concert or movie tickets, a crashed website for a large-scale business may have serious costs. For example, what if the IRS's tax-filing systems went down in early April? What if Amazon's website crashed the week before Christmas?

There are many ways to attack an organization on the basis of availability, but we often hear of availability attacks under the name of "Denial of Service" (DoS) or "Distributed Denial of Service" (DDoS) attacks, which are both attacks where a user (or users, for DDoS) sends multiple Synchronize (SYN) packets to a single webserver Internet Protocol (IP) and overwhelms the request processing capacity of that server, causing it to timeout.

Businesses combat this through techniques such as "load balancing" across armies of servers to handle requests. However, large organizations are not immune from these types of attacks. In 2011, Sony's PlayStation Network (PSN) was taken down repeatedly over several weeks by the hacktivist group Anonymous through DDoS attacks. While it impacted availability, it also seriously eroded customer trust in Sony's PSN system.

Other methods of availability controls are disaster recovery processes, backup/ restoration contingency processes, and network throttling or load balancing across network systems.

APPLICATION, GENERAL, AND KEY CONTROLS

As previously discussed, an IT auditor's primary role is to evaluate the design and operating effectiveness of the IT control environment. There are many ways to define controls. While there are many ways to describe *how* controls protect the environment (we will dissect these views on controls later), there are only two ways to classify *what* the controls protect: **application controls** and **general controls**.

> **Application controls:** Controls that protect the integrity of specific business applications/processes and their associated data from exposure to malicious attackers and ensure the process is completed as intended. These controls are not part of the IT infrastructure.

General controls: Controls that protect the IT environment in which business applications/processes operate, thereby making weaknesses or assurance of these controls applicable to all business applications/processes in the applicable IT environment.

NOTE: *As an example, when testing user access controls, understanding how users gain access to an application's business processes (like approving a batch total) would be an application control. Understanding how users gain access to the operating system and database management system (DBMS) would be a general control.*

It is important to understand that application controls typically protect business *processes* rather than technology, policies, or organizational structures. As such, technological controls used within applications can still be general controls. For example, password enforcement for authenticating to an application does not protect the actual business process, but access to the application that conducts those business processes. As such, the password controls are considered general controls.

A broad understanding of both application controls and general controls are necessary for an IT auditor to be successful and competent. However, one must also understand their deeply dependent relationship and how one supports the other.

Application vs. General Control Example

Suppose an auditor is reviewing logical access controls within a mission-critical system that provides large payments to vendors. They may choose to review administrative access for the operating systems and databases, as well as review how payments to vendors are managed within the payment application.

Administrative access controls may be represented by strong passwords, two-factor authentication, and various logical controls (such as idle account lockouts, incorrect password lockouts, password lifetime, and so on). Additionally, the state of administrative access within the system's operating systems and databases does not *directly* affect the business processes within the application. They affect the access to the *technological components* that supports the application's business processes, but not the processes themselves. As such, these controls are considered general controls.

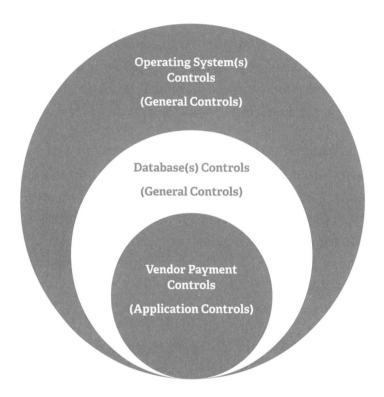

The auditor moves on and sees that the business process of approvals for vendor payments requires a requestor for payment, an approver of payment (that cannot be the requestor), a second approver over a certain amount (that cannot be the requestor or first approver), and a different user to process the payment.

What we see is that there is a clear segregation of duties within the business process. The controls that are enforced around role assignments (requestors, approvers, payers, etc.) and the segregation of duties all directly affect the *business process* of paying vendors. As such, these controls are considered application controls.

Suppose an audit team reviews a mission-critical application and determine that all tested controls are effective. Does that mean that the data the application is using to generate reports can be trusted? On the surface, the answer appears to be "yes," but how can we be sure that the data is protected from corruption, manipulation, etc.?

Think back to our integrity discussion. What if an outside malicious attacker or a malicious insider with administrative access were able to manipulate data in the database that supports the application that was just audited? Despite the strong application controls, the data being used by the application cannot be trusted, so we must gain assurance over the general controls of the IT environment as well.

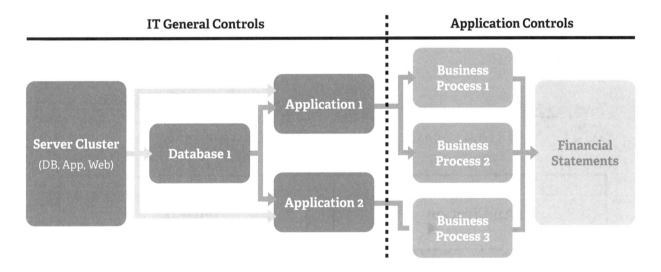

Remember that controls developed in the application itself are general controls—the controls over the business processes the application performs are application controls (such as approval of settlements or prohibiting payments over a certain threshold). This is where the dependency between the control types comes into play because we cannot provide reasonable assurance over our key applications if we cannot also provide reasonable assurance over the general controls of the IT environment in which they operate.

Key Controls

Between the relationship of application and general controls exists a category that resides across both: **key controls**. These controls represent the most critical controls that exist within the organization, with respect to the assurance of reliable financial statements.

> **Key controls:** Controls that are most critical in supporting the overall assurance of an organization's financial health.

Key controls are deemed to be "key" because an ineffective key control can directly result in misstatements of financial data, which can result in inaccurate financial reporting for an organization.

PRIMARY, COMPENSATING, AND MITIGATING CONTROLS

Application			General		
	Key			Key	
Primary	Compensating	Mitigating	Primary	Compensating	Mitigating

Now that we understand general and application controls, we can begin to understand the function of these types of controls. Controls serve a variety of purposes, and they can help create a strong, layered defense for the IT environment. In an ideal world, we would see that all our controls are operating as **primary controls**. For example, an application that has built-in password controls for user accounts would be expected to use that control as its main form of authenticating users to the application. This control was made for this single purpose, so it would (ideally) be needlessly complicated to find other ways to authenticate users to the application.

> **Primary controls:** Controls that operate as the intended control of choice for the technology, application, business process, or organizational structure.

However idealistic an organization may be, most people understand that organizations must be realistic. For example, suppose that the password authentication control built into a mission-critical application cannot allow passwords that are long or complex enough to comply with internal policy. As a result, the organization uses some other authentication method, such as active directory, single sign-on, or Lightweight Directory Access Protocol (LDAP). This allows the organization to comply with their internal security policies on password management while also continuing to use their mission-critical application. The method of control is not the ideal (primary) control, but it accomplishes the goal of strong password enforcement, nonetheless. This is an example of **compensating controls**.

> **Compensating controls:** Controls that accomplish the intended purpose of a primary control when the primary control is unable to perform the controlling action at the level necessary to comply with requirements.

Another example of a compensating control would be within the audit logging and monitoring process. Suppose a system administrator has excessive elevated privileges that allow them to make configuration changes within an application, create user accounts, and assign roles. The system would most likely produce logs of administrator activity. But what if the administrator also had default access to those logs? The primary control would be to revoke access to those logs. However, that may not be feasible if the administrator still needed access to the logs for forensic purposes in the event of a system incident.

Assuming management is aware of this user's elevated privileges, a good compensating control would be for management to ensure that all activities performed by this user are logged and monitored by a separate individual or security team and this user cannot access or modify the logs generated by their activities.

Suppose that an accounting manager within our application performs mission-critical account balancing procedures. While we can imagine that a manager with that level of responsibility is relatively competent, we know humans will make mistakes eventually. Because of this, the application triggers an error alarm when the accounts in the application do not correctly reconcile after a predetermined period and will not allow the manager to post the account balances until the accounts are reconciled.

The alert that signals to the accounting manager that he/she has made an error is an example of a **mitigating control**, which takes the form of either a **preventative** or **detective** control, depending on the context of the situation. This type of control forces the user to correct the mistake and prevents critical errors in the account reporting process. The Internal Revenue Service (IRS) defines mitigating controls as such:

Mitigating controls: Controls that are used to discover and prevent mistakes that may lead to uncorrected and/or unrecorded misstatements. Preventative controls act as safeguards to stop unsatisfactory outcomes from occurring within the environment, while detective controls act as countermeasures to force or alert the user to correct the current state when an unsatisfactory outcome occurs.

Application and general controls can be either primary, compensating, or mitigating controls based on their intended purpose. So, as you continue to learn the nuances associated with controls, remember that application and general controls describe *what* they protect, while primary, compensating, and mitigating controls describe *how* they protect. Additionally, key controls are determined by an auditor while reviewing overall control design and define what controls are most critical to proper operational effectiveness.

CONTROL FAMILIES

IT auditors are metaphorical detectives searching for enough evidence to draw conclusions on a set of facts provided by management. At a high level, we first gain an understanding of an organization's IT environment by interviewing key personnel that are in charge of the various business/IT processes we are auditing. Once we do that, we request various supporting documentation in an effort to verify what we have learned via inquiry. We perform an inspection of policies, procedures, and other documentation to determine if they are sufficient and compliant with various criteria, which we will discuss in a later chapter.

Whether we are talking about an information system or an application, we must approach any audit with the understanding that we need to evaluate the operating system, database, and application layers to conclude on the design and operating effectiveness of the control environment.

However, depending on the scope of an audit or the timeframe allotted, an IT auditor can focus on application-level controls during year one, and IT general controls or infrastructure controls (operating system and database) in year two, as an example. An audit always involves performing testing on the various information technology controls. With respect to Federal IT auditing, the control categories that we review per the Government Accountability Office Federal Information System Control Audit Manual (GAO FISCAM) are as follows:

- **Access controls.** Controls provide reasonable assurance that access to computer resources (data, equipment, and facilities) is reasonable and restricted to authorized individuals, including effective protection of information system boundaries; identification and authentication mechanisms; authorization controls; protection of sensitive system resources; audit and monitoring capability, including incident handling; and physical security controls.

- **Configuration management.** Controls provide reasonable assurance that changes to information system resources are authorized and systems are configured and operated securely and as intended, including effective configuration management policies, plans, and procedures; current configuration identification information, proper authorization, testing, approval, and tracking of all configuration changes; routine monitoring of the configuration; updating software on a timely basis to protect against known vulnerabilities; and documentation and approval of emergency changes to the configuration.

- **Segregation of duties.** Controls provide reasonable assurance that incompatible duties are effectively segregated, including segregation of incompatible duties and responsibilities and related policies, and control of personnel activities through formal operating procedures, supervision, and review.

- **Security management.** Controls provide reasonable assurance that security management is effective, including security management program; periodic assessments and validation of risk; security control policies and procedures; security awareness training and other security-related personnel issues; periodic testing and evaluation of the information security policies, procedures, and practices; remediation of information security weaknesses; and security over activities performed by external third parties.

- **Contingency planning.** Controls provide reasonable assurance that contingency planning (1) protects information resources and minimizes the risk of unplanned interruptions and (2) provides for recovery of critical operations should interruptions occur, including assessment of the criticality and sensitivity of computerized operations and identification of supporting resources; assessment of steps taken to prevent and minimize potential damage and interruption; comprehensive contingency plan; and periodic testing of the contingency plan, with appropriate adjustments to the plan based on the testing.

- **Business process controls.** Business process controls are the automated and/or manual controls applied to business transaction flows and relate to the completeness, accuracy, validity, and confidentiality of transactions and data during application processing. They typically cover the structure, policies, and procedures that operate at a detailed business process (cycle or transaction) level and operate over individual transactions or activities across business processes. Specific types of business process controls are transaction data input relates to controls over data that enter the application (e.g., data validation and edit checks); transaction data processing relates to controls over data integrity within the application (e.g., review of transaction processing logs); transaction data output relates to controls over data output and distribution (e.g., output reconciliation and review); master data setup and maintenance relates to controls over master data, which is the key information that is relatively constant and shared between multiple functions or applications (e.g., vendor file).

- **Interface controls.** Consist of those controls over the (1) timely, accurate, and complete processing of information between applications and other feeder and receiving systems on an ongoing basis, and (2) complete and accurate migration of clean data during conversion.

- **Data management controls.** Are relevant to most business process applications because applications frequently utilize the features of a data management system to enter, store, retrieve, or process information, including detailed, sensitive information such as financial transactions, customer names, and social security numbers. Data management systems include database management systems, specialized data transport/communications software (often called middleware), data warehouse software, and data extraction/reporting software. Data management system controls enforce user authentication/authorization, availability of system privileges, data access privileges, application processing hosted within the data management systems, and segregation of duties.

Other examples of control families can be found in the National Institute of Standards and Technologies (NIST) Special Publication 800-53 (NIST SP

800-53), which contains various IT security control family categories for the federal government and is widely used by organizations looking to establish an industry-accepted benchmark on IT controls. We will review each of these control categories in detail later in this book.

WHAT IS AN INFORMATION SYSTEMS CONTROL?

Let's take access controls, for example. In FISCAM, control IA-5.1 is a control technique that describes the basic requirements of secure password parameters.

Password-based authenticators

- are not displayed when entered;
- are changed periodically (e.g., every 30 to 90 days);
- contain alphanumeric and special characters;
- are sufficiently long (e.g., at least eight characters);
- have an appropriate life (automatically expire);
- are prohibited from reuse for a specified period of time (e.g., at least six generations); and
- are not the same as the user ID.

The respective NIST 800-53 control that relates to this FISCAM control is as follows:

IA-5 (1)(a)	Enforces minimum password complexity of [Assignment: organization-defined requirements for case sensitivity, number of characters, mix of upper-case letters, lowercase letters, numbers, and special characters, including minimum requirements for each type].

IA-5 (1)(b)	Enforces at least the following number of changed characters when new passwords are created: [Assignment: organization-defined number].
IA-5 (1)(c)	Stores and transmits only cryptographically protected passwords.
IA-5 (1)(d)	Enforces password minimum and maximum lifetime restrictions of [Assignment: organization-defined numbers for lifetime minimum, lifetime maximum].
IA-5 (1)(e)	Prohibits password reuse for [Assignment: organization-defined number] generations.
IA-5 (1)(f)	Allows the use of a temporary password for system logons with an immediate change to a permanent password.

You may be asking what the difference is between FISCAM and NIST. Great question! FISCAM is an IT audit methodology that was developed based on NIST for the Federal space, whereas NIST and all of its various publications are the criteria by which FISCAM controls should be assessed. For example, when an external auditor is developing his/her audit work program, which will be discussed in Chapter 4, they should utilize FISCAM. However, when the auditor is testing controls and drafting his/her Notice of Findings and Recommendations (NFR) (also known as an "observation" or "finding"), NIST and its various publications are the criteria or standard by which to perform these tests and document the criteria for those NFRs. This will make more sense as we progress through the material.

In order to test this control technique, an IT auditor must understand the difference between Test of Design (TOD) and Test of Operating Effectiveness (TOE).

TOD involves inquiring with management/process owners to gain an understanding of the process around the specific control we are testing. TOD also involves requesting and obtaining various policy/procedural documentation to determine if the process has been documented and is consistent with what we learned during our inquiry with management/process owner. The auditor must document these inquiry and inspection of policy/procedure results in what is called an "audit workpaper," which we will discuss in more detail in subsequent chapters.

Another important point to note here is the difference between a **policy** and a **procedure**. Auditors must review policies and their respective procedures during the Test of Design (TOD) phase of an audit. Sometimes, auditors may use these interchangeably. However, this is incorrect.

> **Policy:** An entity level document, high-level in nature, which describes the overall governing culture and requirements that apply to the entity as a whole, including staff, management, and oversight bodies.

> **Procedure:** A detailed process document that describes how a control or set of controls should be implemented at a system and/or platform level.

TOE involves observing the control process live, capturing screenshots, obtaining a population of changes or users for example, selecting a sample, and requesting further documentation to determine if the control is operating effectively. For example, if testing "changes," the TOE phase would involve requesting and obtaining a population of changes, selecting a sample based on an approved sampling methodology, and obtaining detailed supporting documentation to determine if these changes were appropriately documented, requested, approved, and tested prior to being deployed into the production environment.

Remember Control IA-5(1), "Password-based Authentication?" In order to perform the test of this control, let's assume users authenticate to Application X by entering a username and password. Control IA-5(1) describes the basic control and/or best practices around password parameters. Thus, we would first interview the administrator of Application X and ask what the password parameters are for Application X (i.e., minimum password length, whether passwords are displayed in plain text when entered, whether passwords are required to be changed periodically, are passwords required to contain alphanumeric and special characters, etc.).

After we document our inquiry, we can ask the Application X administrator to provide us with the policy that describes what the required password parameters should be for Application X. We will then compare the policy to what we learned via inquiring with the Application X admin and ensure there are no inconsistencies.

This analysis is known as Test of Design or "TOD," which we will discuss in a later chapter. The next phase is to perform Test of Effectiveness or "TOE." This is where we will go to the Application X administrator and observe him/her log into Application X to verify the required password length is accurate and that passwords are not displayed when entered. We will then ask the Application X admin to provide us with a screenshot of the password parameters so that we can verify that they are consistent with the analysis we performed in the TOD phase. If everything checks out, you/the auditor can conclude that this control IA-5(1) is "designed" and "operating effectively," with "no exceptions noted."

CHAPTER 3
THE IT AUDIT PROCESS

• •

For those that enjoy consistency and a repeatable process, the **audit process** easily meets those requirements. Aside from the nuances from the type of fieldwork that is performed, the overall process that an auditor undertakes to guide the assessment, observation, and reporting of control evaluation is largely a repeatable process for audit staff.

The repeatable and predictive nature of the process (not the scope of fieldwork) provides much needed stability to the business and audit firm alike. It eliminates the potential for surprises, in terms of how the audit firm plans to conduct its audit, and allows the business and audit firm to engage in the audit process with a collective sense of expectation regarding how each party will conduct themselves.

In this chapter, we will explore each major step and its purpose in the audit process. There are

1. Planning

The Audit Lifecycle

3. Reporting

2. Fieldwork

many organizations that will provide any arbitrary number of steps to the audit process, depending on the granularity desired, but leading organizational bodies, such as the Information Systems Audit and Control Association (ISACA), take the simplistic route, which is how we will cover the audit process. For the purposes of this overview, the audit process, holistically, can be summarized in three major phases: Planning, Fieldwork, and Reporting.

> **Audit process:** The process in which an auditor will plan, perform, and communicate results of prescribed audit work over a business's controls, divided into three phases: Planning, Fieldwork, and Reporting.

The audit process often begins and ends the same way a scientist conducts experiments: with a hypothesis and a conclusion.

An auditor's initial insight into the business, the industry, or the external economic conditions leads them to suspect or anticipate certain areas of the business are riskier than others (the hypothesis). But how can they prove that? By performing fieldwork (testing the hypothesis) and communicating the results (reporting).

PLANNING

The first step in the audit process is to plan the audit. The planning phase allows an auditor to first inform the client of their intentions to perform the audit. This is not to be confused with the official "announcement letter" (more on that later).

A Risk-Based Approach

An audit team will formulate their audit scope as an output of the completed planning phase using a risk-based audit approach. **Risk-based auditing** is the de-facto standard for how an audit team approaches the potential inclusion of business areas into the formal audit scope.

Risk-based auditing: The process of auditing in accordance with what business areas present (or potentially present) the greatest amount of risk to an organization, thereby warranting inclusion to an audit scope or, during fieldwork, greater scrutiny, with respect to the total amount of fieldwork performed.

Risk-based auditing forces the planning phase of an audit to be an in-depth review of critical areas of the business. While this does not include the testing of controls, it requires the auditor to have a deep understanding of important business processes, data sensitivity, mission-critical IT systems, external factors like regulatory requirements or emerging technology, and key dependencies/relationships between business lines.

Risk-based auditing also requires the auditor to maximize the value between the vast potential scope of fieldwork and the value the fieldwork brings to the business. An audit may cover 90 percent of a business's IT systems, but if the most critical systems for the business are part of the missing 10 percent that wasn't audited, the business loses out on a tremendous amount of value. Additionally, it prevents an auditor from meeting the main goal of an audit: assurance over business processes and financial reporting.

Consequently, risk-based approaches to auditing also allow an auditor to minimize the main adversary of successful and reliable business operations: risk. Conceptually, we can imagine that an audit attempts to minimize total audit risk with the following formula:

Audit Risk = Control Risk * Detective Risk * Inherent Risk

Control risk: The risk that a control will not properly protect a business process from improper reporting or processing.

Detective risk: The risk that an auditor will not detect an anomaly in control effectiveness or misstatement of financial information.

Inherent risk: The risk of an error in reporting or process that is not the result of a control deficiency, such as the result of transaction complexity or data sensitivity/dependency.

Audit risk: The risk that material weaknesses in financial reporting or business processes exist, even though an audit opinion attests to the soundness of the respective reporting or processes.

The chief goal of an audit engagement is to reduce the overall risk of the business. An auditor can maximize this likelihood by adopting a risk-based approach to their planning, which ultimately drives the audit scope, fieldwork, and reporting.

Building the Audit Universe

Additionally, auditors will conduct interviews with key stakeholders and management. These formal interviews are taken into consideration to help answer fundamental questions as the auditor attempts to form their "hypothesis" of what is most important or riskiest to the organization.

An auditor must also consider a wide collection of variables that drive the overall determination of the audit scope. It is common for an auditor to review organizational charts, functional overview documents, process flow charts, and other key documentation about the nature of how a business is run. While not an exhaustive list, other major concepts that an auditor must consider when planning an audit are as follows.

Major Concept	Examples
Audit history	Previous audit scopes, previous audit findings, Service Organization Control (SOC) reports
Organizational structure	New management positions, significant organizational changes
Fixed constraints	SOX or fiscal-year reporting requirements, legal requirements
Budget constraints	Billable hours allowed, cost of audit engagement
Staff requirements	Availability, competence/ expertise levels, technical needs
External factors	Industry conditions, technology adoption, economic impacts

These items (and more) should be considered in addition to the potential weaknesses or perceived deficiencies identified during planning. Ultimately, the auditor should aggregate all concepts into what we will call the *Audit*

Universe—all potential areas that could be audited in the business to drive risk down as low as possible through the assurance activities performed in the audit engagement.

Audit Universe

Represents potential range of auditable components, programs, activities, processes, structures, and initiatives

Audit Risk Assessment

During the planning process, audit assigns risk to entity universe with documented reasoning

Audit Scope Ranking

Audit prioritizes risk and determines highest priority

Audit Work

Developing the Audit Scope

Conceptually, we can visualize this planning process as an inverted pyramid, where the more we learn about a business and its riskiest areas, the narrower the audit scope becomes. A risk-based approach will find the balance between audit invasiveness and expanse of scope with the need to maximize value and assurance over a business's operations. Cross-referenced with various factors outlined above, the auditor can then develop the audit scope and move on to the fieldwork phase.

Keeping any existing constraints (budget, staff, etc.) in mind, the auditor would select areas of the organization to audit that present the most potential risk to the business. This can include end-to-end processes, subsets of applications and/or systems, specific historical financial reports, and policy/procedural documentation.

FIELDWORK

The actual process of auditing begins with the fieldwork stage of the audit process. If the planning phase is executed using the risk-based approach and the scope is surgically assigned to maximize value while minimizing unnecessary audit work, then fieldwork will provide the greatest level of assurance possible to a business. Fieldwork is initiated with the issuance of an **announcement letter** (sometimes called an "engagement memo"), which is provided to the business.

> **Announcement letter:** An official letter provided to the business by the auditor that officially announces the beginning of the formal audit engagement. The letter MUST include the audit objectives and scope, auditor responsibilities, and management responsibilities.

In addition to these requirements, the announcement letter will often include the audit staff assigned (and audit engagement leadership) and the timeline for fieldwork and reporting. Like any good contract, the announcement letter sets the stage for the audit engagement, ensures both the auditor and the audited understand expectations during the audit, and creates a formal sense of accountability for both parties.

Announcement Letter	Evidence Request	Analyze Evidence

Collecting Audit Evidence

Once the audit engagement has kicked off, it is time for formal requests for evidence so that fieldwork can commence. For an auditor to evaluate audit evidence, the auditor must first request that evidence. While we will ultimately review specific examples of what constitutes effective audit analysis in this book (see Chapter 4), we will cover the high-level concepts of how we facilitate evidence collection and analysis. An auditor will begin the field process by issuing an **evidence request**.

> **Evidence request:** Pointed, specific, and surgical requests for information in order to accomplish the audit objectives identified in the planning phase.

On the surface, one might think that an evidence request is rather straightforward. In reality, evidence requests will often make or break the fieldwork phase of an audit.

For example, an auditor may be attempting to verify that privileged administrative access provisioning is reasonable for a specific application (we'll call it "Application A"). In this business, access is managed for Applications A, B, C, and D with the same enterprise-level tool. If the auditor submitted an evidence request for an output of all accounts managed with the enterprise tool, the auditor would be reviewing an excessive amount of accounts. The accounts may not be administrative accounts, they may not be part of Application A, and it may take the IT department several hours to compile the data for the request.

In the end, the auditor has wasted time (his/hers and the IT staff's) by requesting irrelevant information. Instead, the evidence request should be for an output of all privileged administrative accounts that have access to Application A only. This type of request is clear in its scope, and the IT staff dedicate only the necessary time to provide this exact evidence. Like our risk-based approach to planning, we minimize invasiveness and we maximize value.

Analyzing Audit Evidence

Reviewing and interpreting audit evidence, when documented well, should read simplistically. While the work and evidence can be extremely complicated, the documentation of the analysis should not. There are several standards for how audit evidence should be documented in **workpapers**, including standards set by Information Systems Audit and Control Association (ISACA), Institute of Internal Auditors (IIA), Yellow Book, or Public Company Accounting Oversight Board (PCAOB). All industry-accepted standards require similar concepts.

> **Workpapers:** Documentation artifacts composed by the audit staff that capture the analysis of audit evidence.

Audit evidence analysis, documented via workpapers, will adhere to the following concepts to ensure it properly shows the correct conclusion of control structures and control effectiveness:

Concept	Detail
Logical	All evidence should be reviewed in a logical, straightforward manner and documented in a way that is easy to interpret and follow.

Concise	All analysis should be relevant. Analysis that later proves to be irrelevant during the fieldwork process should be removed and only include evidence and analysis that supports the control test objective.
Objective	Audit evidence analysis should be devoid of euphemisms and subjective language (e.g., "The current state of this control is really terrible.").
Conclusive	Each workpaper makes a conclusion on the reasonableness of the evidence, not whether something is "right" or "wrong." As such, auditors often conclude their workpapers by including statements such as "No Exceptions Noted" or "Deemed Reasonable."

We will take a deeper dive into the intricacies of reviewing evidence and properly documenting analysis in workpaper in later chapters. When an auditor collects appropriate audit evidence, the auditor should be able to clearly demonstrate, beyond reasonable disagreement, that a control is effective or not.

One major method of ensuring audit fieldwork is properly documented is to have audit leadership review the fieldwork and approve the work. The expectation is that an auditor with the same background and experience should be able to review the audit evidence and reach the same conclusion as the fieldwork auditor, following the documented audit analysis.

Drawing Fieldwork Conclusions

One critical piece of fieldwork analysis is the conclusion of each test step. In the context of audit evidence and workpaper documentation, it is required (from a best-practice standpoint) that an auditor draw a conclusion on the workpapers they have documented. Auditors draw conclusions based on the concept of **reasonable assurance**. That is, since an auditor can't truly have complete knowledge of a process or control (and all possible scenarios that could impact the control), the auditor can say the test shows that the control can reasonably ensure proper outputs. The PCAOB defines it as such:

> **Reasonable assurance:** The assessment of the effectiveness of internal controls ... [including] the understanding that there is a remote likelihood that material misstatements will not be prevented or detected on a timely basis.

Notice that the auditor does not conclude as whether a control is "perfect," or that the control environment is "perfect." The auditor must always leave room for extenuating circumstances and ensure that the business infer this as well. For example, although a password is eighteen characters long and has a combination of complexity rules (numbers, upper/lowercase, special characters), is it still technically possible for an attacker or malicious insider to crack that password? Realistically, probably not. Is it still *literally* possible? Of course—with enough computing power (and a little luck or insider knowledge) the password control could potentially be circumvented. Thus, auditors draw their conclusions through the concept of reasonable assurance.

Assuming no exceptions are found in the control test, auditors will often conclude their workpapers by using phrases like "No Concerns/Exceptions Noted" or "Deemed Reasonable." Once this conclusion is reached and all control tests are complete, the audit team can begin engaging in the reporting phase of the audit engagement.

REPORTING

The reporting phase is the primary output of the audit process for management. Management does not see the documentation of the planning work.

Management does not see the workpapers that are developed in the fieldwork phase. It is only the audit report and associated observations that are presented to management.

The purpose of the audit report is to communicate an **audit opinion**. This audit opinion is used to inform management, shareholders, and other critical stakeholders of the overall state of financial statements and control effectiveness. For many investors, financial statements without an audit report (and subsequent audit opinion) are deemed worthless. Thus, the impact and value of an audit report cannot be understated.

> **Audit opinion:** An auditor's formal, reported opinion as to whether the financial statements are materially reasonable, in accordance with Generally Accepted Accounting Principles (GAAP), and that control structures within are effective.

As fieldwork is completed and workpapers are documented, reporting takes on two major forms: **observations** and **audit reports**. Observations, sometimes called "Notice of Finding and Recommendation" (NFR), are what the layman often refers to as a "finding" in the audit process. While auditing is often referred to as a "science," it is in the reporting phase that an auditor has the freedom to be creative and exercise their auditing skills as an "art."

> **Observation:** Artifact developed by the auditor and presented to management that leverages audit evidence analysis to identify control deficiencies, highlight residual risk, and recommend a course of corrective action.

Audit report: Main audit process output that communicates the overall results of the audit, including any reportable observations and an official audit opinion.

The artifacts produced in the reporting phase rely as much on the basic facts aggregated through fieldwork as it relies on an auditor's creative writing ability—an ability that is necessary to effectively communicate the results of an audit to management in an impactful way.

We will cover audit observations later in this book. But, for now, recognize that observations are the main way that deficiencies are communicated to management post-fieldwork. The subject matter that makes up an official observation is typically communicated the moment that sufficient evidence has been collected to verify the noted weaknesses (usually during the fieldwork phase), giving time for management to understand and respond appropriately to the observation. Only after fieldwork is completed are observations considered for inclusion in the official report.

Reporting Structure

An audit report's structure is largely consistent, regardless of the outcome of the audit, in terms of how it communicates the health of financial statements and control effectiveness. However, there are some nuances, depending on how poor the audit results may be. Let's explore the structure of audit reports.

1. **Required criteria:** There are certain criteria that must be included in the audit report. These items are no different from what was communicated in the official announcement letter: scope, objectives, and criteria.

    Additional criteria include legal references, such as a disclaimer regarding Generally Accepted Auditing Standards (GAAS) usage, independence clauses, etc. These items are included to ensure that stakeholders understand that the audit was conducted in accordance with whatever governing bodies affect the relevant audit practices (such as IIA, PCAOB, Yellow Book, and so on). There are industry-accepted requirements for audit reporting writing, such as the AICPA's AU-508 publication on audit report requirements.

2. **Assurance of opinion:** The report must include certain statement(s) of assurance that the auditor can opine on the financial statements and associated controls with reasonable accuracy, based purely on the evidence reviewed during the fieldwork phase of the audit.

3. **Observations:** The "findings" of the audit, this section includes all noted weaknesses and management's official responses to the weaknesses, which include remediation plans and timelines. Additionally, management will have previously provided an official response to any observations, and those responses will be included.

4. **Audit opinion:** The most important part of the report, this is the auditor's opinion on the health of the financial statements of the organization that was audited. The audit opinion is also clarified with Generally Accepted Accounting Principles (GAAP), for the purposes of consistency and industry-accepted accounting practices.

The audit report contains a single audit opinion, which is communicated as one of three major opinion categories (plus a fourth extenuating situation):

1. **Unqualified:** This opinion means that no material weaknesses were discovered during the audit and that there is reasonable assurance that the organization is operating effectively and truthfully, with respect to their financial statements and control structure.

2. **Qualified:** This opinion means that, except for identified weaknesses (noted in the observations within the report), there is reasonable assurance that the organization is operating effectively and truthfully, with respect to their financial statements and control structure.

3. **Adverse:** A rare audit opinion, this opinion means that the financial statements do not reasonably attest to the financial well-being and/or the control structure is ineffective. These opinions often are the result of material misstatements, fraud, or gross mismanagement of an organization's assets.

4. **Disclaimer of opinion:** This opinion means that an auditor cannot or will not express an audit opinion for management. Often, a disclaimer is issued if a company's practices prevent the auditor from obtaining sufficient evidence to form an opinion, or other changes in a company's operating structure or processes prevent sufficient audit evidence from being obtained. Reasons for the disclaimer should be included in the audit report.

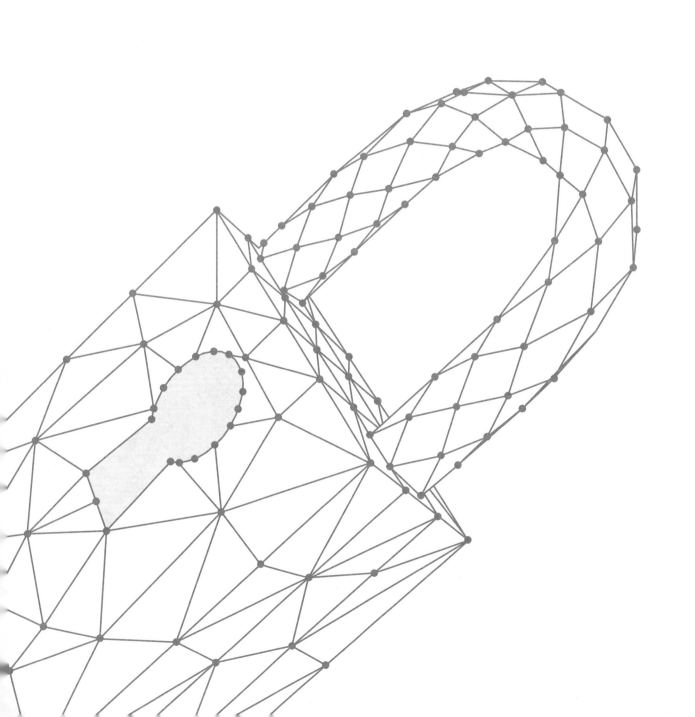

CHAPTER 4
WORKPAPER DEVELOPMENT

• •

While each phase of the audit process is essential and relies upon the full skillset of an auditor, the workpaper documentation within the fieldwork phase is what one often associates with the "core" work of an auditor. It is the main output of the actual analysis of audit evidence and where conclusions are drawn that ultimately drive the formulation of audit observations. While we will cover more advanced forms of workpaper documentation around sampling in later chapters, we will cover the main structure of how workpapers are documented here.

We have already covered how an auditor plans the scope of their audit and how audit evidence is obtained in Chapter 3. For the purposes of Chapter 4, let's assume that effective evidence requests were submitted to management and the evidence supplied is sufficient to draw reasonable conclusions.

To recap, we should remember that audit evidence analysis should follow the four major themes: *logical, concise, objective,* and *conclusive.* Working from those four concepts, our workpapers should be documented to convey the proper conclusion, based on the evidence provided.

Workpaper Structure

When developing workpaper structure, we always develop them with the following "drill down" formula: *Audit Objective > Control Objective > Control > Test*. This methodology allows the auditor to ensure that all work goes to support the audit objectives of the engagement. The value derived from an audit would exponentially drop (or disappear entirely) if the actual tests of controls do not support control objectives and overall audit objectives. See the example below about testing administrative access:

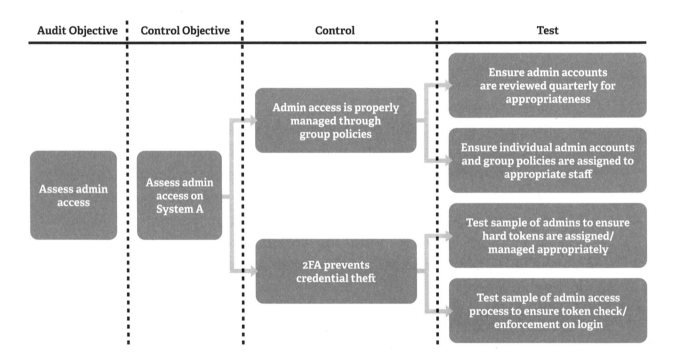

Audit Objective	Control Objective	Control	Test
Assess admin access	Assess admin access on System A	Admin access is properly managed through group policies	Ensure admin accounts are reviewed quarterly for appropriateness
			Ensure individual admin accounts and group policies are assigned to appropriate staff
		2FA prevents credential theft	Test sample of admins to ensure hard tokens are assigned/managed appropriately
			Test sample of admin access process to ensure token check/enforcement on login

Workpaper Template: Components

- **Purpose:** This section of the workpaper always starts with "To determine if XXXX." The "XXXX" should be populated by the actual control activities in FISCAM being assessed.

- **Source:** This is where all supporting documentation/artifacts are assessed in order to come to the conclusion noted in the workpaper, linked, and documented. Information, such as date received, who provided the information, and full title of the document should be included.

- **Scope:** This is where all of relevant FISCAM control techniques would be noted or listed.

- **Testing procedures:** This is where all of the TOD and/or TOE procedures that are documented in the audit work program will be listed, along with the content/results of the testing. It is recommended to have separate TOD and TOE workpapers and conclude the TOD first prior to moving into TOE. Note that if TOD fails, it is NOT necessary to test TOE until the TOD failures have been remediated by the audited client.

- **Conclusion:** This is where the auditor will note if controls are effective or not effective.

The header or footer of the document should contain the workpaper number. Numbering or naming workpapers can use the controls they are targeting. For example, a workpaper reviewing security management policies and procedures would be "WP X-SM-1.1."

Testing Example

The high-level audit objective (communicated in the announcement letter) is to assess administrative privileges within the organization. A practical approach to meeting that objective is to assess it on systems within the organization. Assuming we adopted a risk-based approach, we would say that System A is a mission-critical system and, thus, warrants inclusion to support the audit objective. Having effective controls in System A for administrative access would greatly reduce the control risk to the organization and, as such, represents our *control objective*.

Once we have identified a system to be tested, we then consider how to assess administrative access on System A. While there can be many ways to perform this assessment, for this example, we have chosen to verify effectiveness of logical access coding of the application and two-factor authentication (2FA) mechanisms. Each of these represent an actual *control*, or a safeguard/countermeasure for ensuring System A will operate in a certain manner.

How do we test those controls to ensure that they are operating effectively? This is where the auditor has designed a test of the controls. The assumption of tests goes like this:

The test is where the auditor will document their fieldwork in accordance with the concepts discussed in Chapter 3. An auditor will document a test by inspecting, inquiring, or sampling the expected result of the business process to ensure that the result is just that—expected. If an auditor receives an unexpected result, it begins to paint a picture of the control itself being ineffective and often warrants additional investigation. We call this unexpected result an **exception**.

Exception: Any deviation or unexpected result encountered during the testing of control activities that indicate the existence of a breakdown in control or process effectiveness.

Maybe the unexpected result was a fluke? A system glitch? A simple oversight? Or maybe the unexpected result was because of more significant issues, such as faulty coding or ineffective application processing or improper tool integration. Understanding the "why" of these unexpected results will help drive a better understanding of potential observations and the subsequent audit report.

Ultimately, these categories, when presented together, represent what we call an **audit program**, which places emphasis on an area of audit attention and encapsulates the overarching test strategies of the auditor. An audit may have several audit programs: one revolving around privileged access management audit work and another around configuration management of mission-critical databases. These collections of audit programs represent the audit work being performed during the fieldwork phase of the audit lifecycle.

> **Audit program:** A set of procedures and objectives that an auditor must follow for the purposes of meeting audit objectives, containing audit workpapers and their subsequent control tests.

In our administrative access example, we would test to see that all administrative account permissions are assigned through a group policy instead of individual roles assigned to them (group management is a best practice in most systems). To test it, we may request an output of all relevant administrative accounts on the system. Then, we may ask for the group membership settings of the administrative group. Last, we may review each administrative account to ensure they are appropriate, and that all accounts within the administrative group are appropriate.

Our expected result is that all administrator accounts are appropriate and accounted for. Additionally, we would expect to see that membership to the administrative group only contains administrative accounts. A deviation from that result would be a user who is not an administrator with an administrative account, or a user assigned to the administrative group who is not an administrator.

Expected Result	Unexpected Result

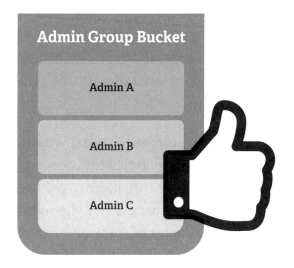 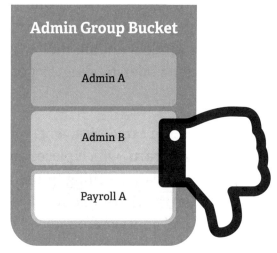

Either situation (group or individual) that produces deviations would infer that the management of administrative access through group policies is not particularly effective, depending on how pervasive unexpected results are.

Workpaper Template Example

As an auditor, suppose you are tasked with developing a workpaper template to guide your testing of controls in the fieldwork phase of the audit lifecycle. What basic items should you include in your workpaper structure to ensure the audit is documented appropriately and ultimately supports your audit objectives? *Note: If you are working at a reputable consulting or accounting firm, they will have all of these templates available; however, we wanted to share some best practices for a workpaper template. This is by all means not the standard you may be using, but is a good example.*

Each individual workpaper is a representation of each individual test that was identified to verify effective controls. In our previous example, one workpaper would contain all audit evidence analysis for one of the tests.

Think back to our basic overview of how audit evidence documentation should be structured. Practically speaking, a simple (but not exhaustive) breakdown of general concepts for documenting your analysis is as follows.

Concept	Detail
Reference testing procedures	Ensure that the content of the workpaper addresses the testing procedures precisely.
Precise reporting	Be precise when citing meetings by including the date of the meeting and links to the meeting minutes in the body of the workpaper. These links should also be in the "source" section of the workpaper along with all other artifacts used.
Accurate assessment terms	Ensure that you utilize proper audit workpaper documentation terminology, such as "inquired," "inspected," "observed," "determined," "reviewed," "obtained."
Precise references	When referencing page numbers in the workpaper, make sure you state "Page X of XX" so the reader knows if you are using the page number of the document or the PDF page number.
Clarity/accuracy	• Make sure all links work • Use the name and title of persons when first referenced • Acronyms defined at first use • Spell check • Spell out numbers one through nine • Consistent use of third-person point of view (for objectivity)

Workpaper/program consistency	Make sure all test steps in the workpapers and programs are consistent.
Fact-based documentation	All factual statements require reference(s).
Conclusion	All results have a documented conclusion that abides by the principle of "reasonable assurance."

Example scenario of an IT audit of a database authentication control test:

Control

Account management settings for System A's database ensure that user authentication is reasonably protected from unauthorized access.

Control Test

Evaluate the controls surrounding end-user authentication for System A's database and determine reasonableness. Consider the following controls:

- Password complexity
- Password age (forced change)
- Password history (reuse)
- Password lock time
- Maximum login attempts

Test Analysis

Auditor interviewed DBA John Smith onsite on [date], where auditor viewed DBA Smith query and provided an output of authentication and password settings for all database-user accounts in the database instance. This query is contained in the file "FILENAME.docx." Auditor reviewed this query output and noted that current authentication settings are:

```
CREATE PROFILE my_profile LIMIT
    FAILED_LOGIN_ATTEMPTS 3 -- Account locked after 3 failed logins.
    PASSWORD LENGTH 18 -- Number of characters for the password.
    PASSWORD NUM 3 -- Requires at least 3 numeric characters.
    PASSWORD SPECIAL 1 -- Requires at least 1 special character.
    PASSWORD UPPER 1 -- Requires at least 1 uppercase alpha character.
    PASSWORD LOWER 1 -- Requires at least 1 lowercase alpha character.
    PASSWORD_LOCK_TIME 5 -- Number of days account is locked for.
    PASSWORD_LIFE_TIME 90 -- Password expires after 90 days.
    PASSWORD_REUSE_MAX 10 -- The number of changes required before
    a password can be reused.
/
```

Auditor determined that these settings are appropriate and in compliance with internal policy and industry best practices. No concerns noted.

Note: *One major thing to remember when reviewing workpapers and audit work programs is to remember that audit work requires paying attention to the "chain reaction." For example, if you change a testing procedure in the workpaper or a conclusion, etc., you must ensure that your audit work program has been updated as well, since you will most likely be linking your workpaper and documenting the overall conclusion of your testing results in the Audit Work Program (AWP).*

Workpaper Self-Review Checklist

- Ensure that the content of the workpaper addresses the testing procedures precisely.

- Be precise when citing meetings by including the date of the meeting and links to the meeting minutes in the body of the workpaper. These links should also be in the source section of the workpaper along with all other artifacts.

- Ensure that you utilize proper audit workpaper documentation terminology, such as "Inquired," "Inspected," "Observed," "Determined," "Reviewed," "Obtained."

- When referencing page numbers in the workpaper, make sure you state "Page X of XX" so the reader knows if you are using the PDF page number or the page number in the actual document as these numbers tend to be different.

- Make sure all links work.

- Make sure all test steps in the workpaper and Audit Work Program (AWP) are consistent.

- Use the name and title of a person when first referenced.

- Spell out acronyms on first use.

- All factual statements require reference.

- Consistent use of third-person point of view for objectivity.

- Spell check the document.

- Spell out numbers one through nine.

- All results should have "Exception Noted" or "No Exception Noted."

CHAPTER 5
WRITING OBSERVATIONS

• •

As an auditor conducts fieldwork and assesses audit evidence provided by the business, exceptions may occur (as discussed in our Chapter 4 "Testing Example"). As these exceptions are noted, the auditor will draft the most important part of their audit: the **observation**. Remember from earlier chapters how we define observations:

> **Observation:** Artifact developed by the auditor and presented to management that leverages audit evidence analysis to identify control deficiencies, highlight residual risk, and recommend a course of corrective action.

Observations go by many names: Finding, Notice of Finding and Recommendation (NFR), Management Point, etc. Regardless of what you name it, an observation is meant to drive and effect change within an organization to improve control and reporting structures. In addition to the announcement letter and the audit report, observations are typically the only artifacts that a client will receive during the audit lifecycle. In light of this, it is essential that auditors draft observations that *matter* to the client. After all, if the observation doesn't drive change for the better, what was the point of the control testing?

UNDERSTANDING THE PURPOSE
OF OBSERVATIONS

A Notice of Finding and Recommendation (NFR) is a document that details one or more conditions or exceptions that have been identified in an audit. If, for example, we determined during Segregation of Duties (SOD) testing that incompatible duties have not been identified by management for a key financial system, this would be a "condition" in the NFR. The other components of an NFR are as follows:

- **Condition:** This is the exception that has been identified.

- **Criteria:** This section should include the relevant NIST criteria and other key guidance such as FISMA, Yellow Book, Green Book, OMB A130, etc. Please note, FISCAM is an audit methodology and NOT CRITERIA. Thus, you cannot use FISCAM as criteria in an NFR.

- **Cause:** This section should be populated after inquiring with management or key process owners on the reason why this exception is present. In this case, we would first need to ask management, "Why haven't you identified incompatible duties? Wouldn't that be critical in determining what roles should be segregated to ensure that all users have access based on least privilege and minimize the risk of fraud?"

- **Consequence/effect:** This section is usually up to the auditor to determine and is subjective. However, if the objective is a financial statement audit, the effect should address the impact to the financial statements.

- **Recommendation:** This section is also subjective to the auditor's perspective and is the most important section of the NFR, as it will provide the most value to upper management with respect to the specific actions that should be taken to resolve this issue.

- **Management response and signature:** This is where management should either concur or not concur with the NFR. Occasionally, auditors will identify an exception and submit an NFR without fully consulting with management, or sometimes there is a communication error whereby a simple document is not provided to the auditor, despite being readily available when the auditor initially requested it. In this case, management would probably not concur with the finding and provide the missing document to satisfy the exception.

Audit observations can take many forms but must always include the five concepts listed above. To see what these concepts looks like when they are properly documented, let us examine some examples of observations, one in a narrative format and one in a tabular format.

Narrative Yellow Book Example

Department of XYZ
System Security Audit
Potential Management Observation

Observation #X

AUDIT AREA: Warehouse Inventory Management System (WIMS) Web Application

TO: XYZ Management

SUBJECT: **Possible Management Observation**

We have identified certain practices or conditions that **are being considered for inclusion in your audit report**. Please review the finding below and provide us with a written response as to whether you believe the facts are correct.

TITLE: Improve the Warehouse Inventory Management System (WIMS) security.

FINDING:

The Department of XYZ (XYZ) does not properly secure their WIMS Web Application. Web Application Environment configuration is essential in the protection of organization assets and sensitive data. This system monitors the inventory levels of controlled substances and is publicly facing making it more vulnerable to attacks. It is imperative that the data in this system upholds integrity and availability. During our review, we noted the following weaknesses:

- XYZ does not appropriately configure application password controls. NIST 800-53 (NIST), Section IA-5, and Internal Policy require that passwords be sufficiently complex to avoid potential authentication breaches. Failure to enforce appropriate password complexity can result in the increased likelihood of unauthorized access.

- XYZ does not properly maintain a baseline configuration document. NIST 800-53, Section CM-2, and Internal Policy require that organizations develop, document, and maintain under configuration control a current baseline configuration. Failure to maintain and enforce an appropriate configuration baseline can result in the increased likelihood of a loss of critical data during an incident or disaster scenario. A properly developed baseline configuration provides a reference point for the web application when development is ongoing.

- XYZ does not appropriately manage user sessions in the application. NIST, Section SC-23, and Internal Policy establishes requirements for communications sessions in ongoing identities of other parties and in the validity of information transmitted. Failure to implement appropriate session ID management controls can result in the increased likelihood of being exploited by session hijacking by an attacker attempting to gain access.

We determined that these weaknesses were the result of a failure to respond to developments in the technological landscape. The application, originally developed in 20XX-5, lacks appropriate expertise to effectively manage and secure due to its antiquated nature. Additionally, XYZ does not have a staff member with the expertise to submit an RFP.

We recommend that XYZ evaluate and implement an application solution (including potential Commercial Off The Shelf (COTS) products) that will address the concerns noted above in a manner that ensures effective business operations and compliance to NIST 800-53 and applicable internal policies.

Tabular FISCAM NFR Template Example

AGENCY NAME
FISCAL YEAR [DATE] FINANCIAL STATEMENT AUDIT
NOTIFICATION OF FINDING AND RECOMMENDATION (NFR)
NFR #[NUMBER] [SYSTEM NAME – HIGH LEVEL SUBJECT OF NFR]

DATE

NFR Condition	Applicable Criteria
The XXX SYSTEM is currently operating without an ATO. XXX SYSTEM is in Step 2 (Select Security Controls) of the RMF process and is attempting to obtain an ATO. Additionally, [SYSTEM NAME] currently does not have a documented SSP, SAR, or POA&M.	Department of Defense (DoD) Instruction (DoDI) No. 8510.01, *Risk Management Framework (RMF) for DoD Information Technology (IT)*, Section 3 states: It is DoD policy that: a. All DoD [Information Systems] IS and [platform IT] PIT systems must be categorized in accordance with Committee on National Security Systems Instruction (CNSSI) 1253 (Reference (e)), implement a corresponding set of security controls from NIST SP 800-53 (Reference (f)), and use assessment procedures from NIST SP 800-53A (Reference (g)) and DoD-specific assignment values, overlays, implementation guidance, and assessment procedures found on the Knowledge Service (KS) at https://rmfks.osd.mil.

b. Each DoD IS, DoD partnered system, and PIT system must have an authorizing official (AO) responsible for authorizing the system's operation based on achieving and maintaining an acceptable risk posture

c. A plan of action and milestones (POA&M) must be developed and maintained to address known vulnerabilities in the IS or PIT system

d. Continuous monitoring capabilities will be implemented to the greatest extent possible.

NIST SP 800-53, Rev. 4, Section CA-1, "Security Assessment and Authorization Policy and Procedures," states:

"Control: The organization:

a. Develops, documents, and disseminates to [Assignment: organization-defined personnel or roles]:

1. A security assessment and authorization policy that addresses purpose, scope, roles, responsibilities, management commitment, coordination among organizational entities, and compliance; and

2. Procedures to facilitate the implementation of the security assessment and authorization policy and associated security assessment and authorization controls; and

b. Reviews and updates the current:

1. Security assessment and authorization policy [Assignment: organization-defined frequency]; and

2. Security assessment and authorization procedures [Assignment: organization-defined frequency]."

NIST SP 800-53, Rev. 4, Section CA-6, "Security Authorization," states:

"Control: The organization:

a. Assigns a senior-level executive or manager as the authorizing official for the information system;

b. Ensures that the authorizing official authorizes the information system for processing before commencing operations; and

c. Updates the security authorization [Assignment: organization-defined frequency]."

AUDITEE has not performed an access recertification of all XXX SYSTEM user accounts to verify that the users still need access based on job function and least privilege. Additionally, policies and procedures related to performing access recertifications have not been developed or documented.	Department of Defense (DoD) Instruction (DoDI) No. 8510.01, *Risk Management Framework (RMF) for DoD Information Technology (IT)*, states: "It is DoD policy that: a. All DoD Information Systems (IS) and platform IT (PIT) systems must be categorized in accordance with Committee on National Security Systems Instruction (CNSSI) 1253 (Reference [e]), implement a corresponding set of security controls from National Institute of Standards and Technology (NIST) Special Publication (SP) 800-53 (Reference [f]), and use assessment procedures from NIST SP 800-53A (Reference [g]) and DoD-specific assignment values, overlays, implementation guidance, and assessment procedures found on the Knowledge Service (KS) at https://rmfks.osd.mil."

	NIST SP 800-53, Revision (Rev.) 4, *Security and Privacy Controls for Federal Information Systems and Organizations*, Section AC-2, "Account Management," states:
	"Control: The organization:
	j. Reviews accounts for compliance with account management requirements [*Assignment: organization-defined frequency*]."
	NIST SP 800-53, Rev. 4, *Security and Privacy Controls for Federal Information Systems and Organizations*, Section AC-6, "Least Privilege," states:
	"Control: The organization employs the principle of least privilege, allowing only authorized access for users (or processes acting on behalf of users) which are necessary to accomplish assigned tasks in accordance with organizational missions and business functions."
	Control Enhancement 7, "Least Privilege | Review of User Privileges," states:
	"The organization:
	a. Reviews [*Assignment: organization-defined frequency*] the privileges assigned to [*Assignment: organization-defined roles or classes of users*] to validate the need for such privileges; and
	b. Reassigns or removes privileges, if necessary, to correctly reflect organizational mission/business needs.
AUDITEE/AGENCY did not develop, document, and implement policies and procedures that outline SoD requirements for the XXX SYSTEM. Additionally, there is no formal documentation for XXX SYSTEM regarding incompatible activities and transactions that would constitute SoD conflicts for system users.	Department of Defense (DoD) Instruction (DoDI) No. 8510.01, *Risk Management Framework (RMF) for DoD Information Technology (IT)*, states:
	"It is DoD policy that:
	b. All DoD Information Systems (IS) and platform IT (PIT) systems must be categorized in accordance with Committee on National Security Systems Instruction (CNSSI) 1253 (Reference [e]), implement a corresponding set of security controls from National Institute of Standards and Technology (NIST) Special Publication (SP) 800-53 (Reference [f]), and use assessment procedures from NIST SP 800-53A (Reference [g]) and DoD-specific assignment values, overlays, implementation guidance, and assessment procedures found on the Knowledge Service (KS) at https://rmfks.osd.mil."
	NIST SP 800-53, Rev. 4, *Security and Privacy Controls for Federal Information Systems and Organizations*, Section AC-1, "Access Control Policy and Procedures," states:
	"Control: The organization:
	a. Develops, documents, and disseminates to [*Assignment: organization-defined personnel or roles*]:
	1. An access control policy that addresses purpose, scope, roles, responsibilities, management commitment, coordination among organizational entities, and compliance; and
	2. Procedures to facilitate the implementation of the access control policy and associated access controls; and
	b. Reviews and updates the current:
	1. Access control policy [*Assignment: organization-defined frequency*]; and

2.   Access control procedures [*Assignment: organization-defined frequency*]."

NIST SP 800-53, Rev. 4, *Security and Privacy Controls for Federal Information Systems and Organizations*, Section AC-5, "Separation of Duties," states:

"Control: The organization:

a.   Separates [*Assignment: organization-defined duties of individuals*];

b.   Documents separation of duties of individuals; and

c.   Defines information system access authorizations to support separation of duties."

The Government Accountability Office's (GAO) Green Book, dated September 2014, Principles 10.12 through 10.14, *Segregation of Duties*, states:

"10.12 Management considers segregation of duties in designing control activity responsibilities so that incompatible duties are segregated and, where such segregation is not practical, designs alternative control activities to address risk.

10.13 Segregation of duties helps prevent fraud, waste, and abuse in the internal control system. Management considers the need to separate control activities related to authority, custody, and accounting of operations to achieve adequate segregation of duties. Segregation of duties can address the risk of management override. Management override circumvents existing control activities and increases fraud risk. Management addresses this risk through segregation of duties, but cannot absolutely prevent it because of the risk of collusion, where two or more employees act together to commit fraud.

10.14 If segregation of duties is not practical within an operational process because of limited personnel or other factors, management designs alternative control activities to address the risk of fraud, waste, or abuse in the operational process."

In addition, GAO's Green Book, dated September 2014, Principle 11.14, *Segregation of Duties*, states:

"11.14 Management designs control activities to limit user access to information technology through authorization control activities such as providing a unique user identification or token to authorized users. And these control activities may restrict authorized users to the applications or functions commensurate with their assigned responsibilities, supporting an appropriate segregation of duties."

XXX SYSTEM has not fully implemented CUECs for all external information systems.	NIST SP 800-53, Rev. 4, Section SA-9 EXTERNAL INFORMATION SYSTEM SERVICES, states:
	
	"Control: The organization:
	
	   a. Requires that providers of external information system services comply with organizational information security requirements and employ [*Assignment: organization-defined security controls*] in accordance with applicable federal laws, Executive Orders, directives, policies, regulations, standards, and guidance;
	
	   b. Defines and documents government oversight and user roles and responsibilities with regard to external information system services; and

      c.   Employs [*Assignment: organization-defined processes, methods, and techniques*] to monitor security control compliance by external service providers on an ongoing basis."

Office of Management and Budget (OMB) Circular No. A-123, *Management's Responsibility for Enterprise Risk Management and Internal Control,* Section III.B.B1. Service Organizations (pages 24-25) states:

"The Green Book provides internal control considerations for service organizations (shared service providers (SSP) are one example). Service organization internal control considerations include management's responsibility for the performance of third-party provided processes, establishing 'user controls' at the Agency receiving services, and service organization oversight.

- **Management's Responsibility for the Processes Performed by Third-Party Service Organizations.** Third-party service providers perform activities for many agencies. Examples include, but are not limited to: accounting and payroll processing, employee benefit plan servicing, information technology services, protections for sensitive Agency data, acquisition or procurement services, security services, asset management, health care claims processing, and loan servicing. Agencies are ultimately responsible for the services and processes provided by third-party service organizations as they relate to the Agency's ability to maintain internal control over operations, reporting, and compliance with laws and regulations.

- **Management's Responsibility for Establishing User Controls.** If the processes provided by the third-party service organization is significant to an Agency's internal control objectives, then the Agency is responsible for establishing user Agency controls that complement the service organization's controls. Management still retains overall responsibility and accountability for all controls related to the processes provided by the third party, and must monitor the process to make sure it is effective."

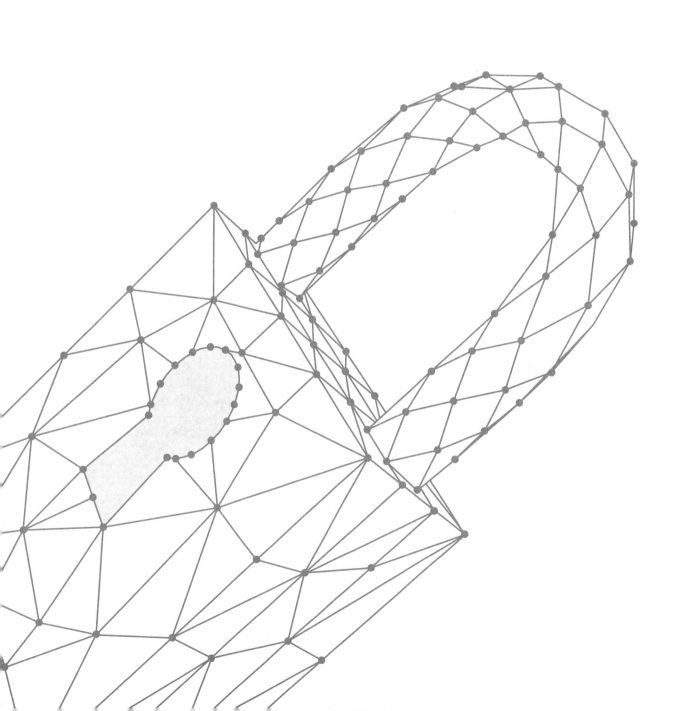

CHAPTER 6

STANDARDS AND BEST-PRACTICES

• •

As we previously mentioned in the audit lifecycle, consistency and predictability are strong advantages for both the auditor and the client being audited. It ensures that both parties understand how the audit process will be conducted and how conclusions will be communicated and reported. This eliminates the "guesswork" of critical points of the audit process and reporting artifacts that will often cause a business's stock price or investor relations to be significantly affected.

But what should govern the audit process? Depending on the relationship of the auditing entity, there are several governing structures that ensure an audit complies with regulatory and industry accepted best practices. These structures are traditionally referred to as audit standards, and for publicly traded companies, they take the form of Generally Accepted Auditing Standards (GAAS), managed by the Auditing Standards Board (ASB) of the American Institute of Certified Public Accountants (AICPA).[1] These standards create a set of guiding principles for auditors to ensure that all aspects of the audit

---

1   https://www.aicpa.org/Research/Standards/AuditAttest/DownloadableDocu-
    ments/AU-00150.pdf

lifecycle are conducted in a manner that warrants trust and confidence in the audit results.

> **Generally Accepted Auditing Standards (GAAS):** Standards that provide guidelines and instructions for the audit lifecycle, which ensures consistent, high-quality, reliable and trustworthy audit work and reporting.

In addition to these GAAS guidelines, there are several other governing bodies within the industry that provide additional guidance for conducting audit work. The Institute of Internal Auditors (IIA) maintains its own set of standards, both for attribute standards (how to define entities and organizational structures) and performance standards (how to perform audit work and report on results).[2]

The PCAOB also leverages the AICPA ASB's GAAS requirements and has adopted a revised structure for communicating those standards into topical categories.[3]

GAAS Overview

GAAS can be broken down into three major concepts: general standards, fieldwork and reporting. Let us examine the major ideas behind these concepts.

---

2   https://na.theiia.org/standards-guidance/Public%20Documents/IPPF-Standards-2017.pdf

3   https://pcaobus.org/Rulemaking/Docket040/Release_2015_002_Reorganization.pdf

General Standards Overview		
Note	**Concept**	**Description**
1	**Competency**	Auditors must be reasonably trained, knowledgeable, and otherwise capable of performing appropriately sufficient audit work.
2	**Independence and objectivity**	Auditors must conduct themselves in a manner that avoids potentially compromising relationships, conflicts of interest, and otherwise avoid situations that would negatively impact their objectivity.
3	**Due care**	Auditors must exercise good, professional judgment and produce work of quality, correctly reporting, in good faith the results of their audit work in the official audit report.

Fieldwork Standards Overview		
Note	**Concept**	**Description**
1	**Planning**	Auditors must sufficiently and appropriately plan an audit and its subsequent scope in a manner consistent with the organizational audit plan (for internal audit) or consistent with appropriate testing over financial controls and related IT systems (external audit).
2	**Competency and knowledge**	Auditors must gain reasonable and sufficient knowledge of the entity's internal control structures, so auditors may appropriately define and execute critical audit procedures, such as material misstatement thresholds, sampling metrics, the identification of fraud, etc.
3	**Evidence**	Auditors must obtain sufficient evidence for reaching an accurate and appropriate conclusion with regard to the health of an entity's financial statements and its internal control structures.

Reporting Standards Overview		
Note	**Concept**	**Description**
1	**GAAS attestation**	Auditors must state whether the audit was conducted in accordance with Generally Accepted Auditing Standards (GAAS). In extenuating circumstances, where GAAS cannot be followed, auditors must disclose those situations and GAAS principles.
2	**Audit opinion**	As previously discussed in the Audit Lifecycle, auditors must disclose one of four "opinions": Qualified (no major issues in audit but some minor issues), Unqualified (no issues in audit), Adverse (major issues in audit), and No Opinion (circumstances result in auditors being unable to reach a conclusion).

Other Common Auditing Standards

GAAS provides the major building blocks of any auditor guidance. However, there are other situations and functions of auditing that require additional guidance. In addition to FISCAM (previously discussed), other common auditing frameworks are Yellow Book and Institute of Internal Auditors (IIA) Standards.

Yellow Book standards drive the audit work of government auditors and auditors performing work for government agencies, including federal and state government. IIA Standards recognize the relationship of an internal audit to the organization and provides additional guidance for the responsibilities and structures of an internal auditing department.

Industry Best-Practices

In addition to auditing standards, there are also concepts used throughout finance, IT, procurement, and other business operations to ensure consistent and effective management of critical business functions. These concepts are commonly called **Industry Best-Practices (IBPs)**. For the purposes of this book, we will focus on IBPs for Information Technology (IT).

It is important to note that the IBPs referenced in this book are not an exhaustive list, but are the commonly referenced best-practices and "company-neutral," in that larger, well-known organizations typically adopt these IBPs and recognize them as appropriate management tools.

1. **Center for Internet Security (CIS) Critical Security Controls (CSCs):** CIS maintains a list of what industry experts consider to be the most at-risk business functions for most business industries. Some CSCs are the result of conceptual understanding of IT operations. For example, as of 2019, the top two controls have traditionally been (1) keep an accurate inventory of hardware and (2) keep an accurate inventory of software. These remain the top two because you must know what hardware and software assets you own, or you cannot protect what you do not know you own. Other concepts include administrative access privileges, security audit logging, secure configurations, etc.

2. **National Institute for Standards and Technology (NIST) Special Publication (SP) 800-53:** Commonly referred to as NIST or NIST 800-53, these standards were created

for benchmark security program implementation for US federal government adoption. Consequently, many private-sector businesses adopted these standards as a means of "speaking apples to apples" with the federal government. It made it easier for businesses to earn contracts because their security standards were set up in the same manner as the federal government. NIST 800-53 makes up the backbone of our FISCAM testing methodologies, which are discussed later in this book. It is divided by control families (e.g., "Access Controls" is defined as "AC"), control types, and control enhancements for highly sensitive situations. Standards defined in NIST 800-53 may require the adoption of an access control program and policy (AC-1, AC-2), as well as processes for assessing appropriateness of access control implementation (various AC controls).

3. **Control Objectives for Information and Related Technologies (COBIT5):** COBIT5 is the fifth iteration of the COBIT framework, which provides guiding principles for adopting and implementing control structures within an entity's business and related IT operations. The Information Systems Audit and Control Association (ISACA) developed COBIT in 1996 and has continued to update the framework ever since. The framework leverages two major concepts: principles and enablers. Principles are the guiding ideas that the business aims to achieve (e.g., meeting stakeholder needs), while enablers are the tools that allow the business to achieve those principles (e.g., policies, process, and information).

A business may choose to adopt one or more of the IBPs, but we must always expect an auditor to conduct themselves and the audit within the boundaries of GAAS. While auditors may leverage the concepts found in these IBPs, they will ultimately need to be adopted within the audit lifecycle.

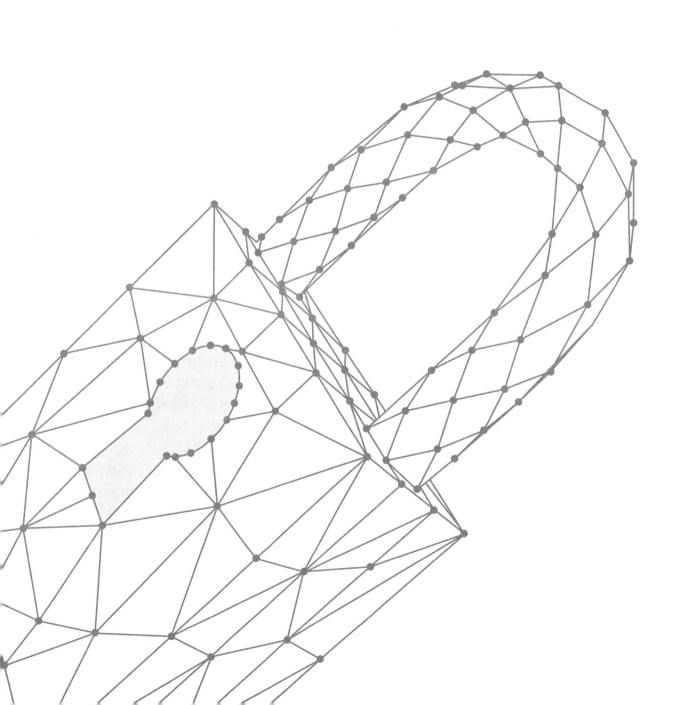

CHAPTER 7
THE PBC LIST

The PCB list ("provided by client") is a listing of all supporting documentation, meetings, and other artifacts that are being requested from the audited client by the auditor to document and complete the audit work. After the kick-off meeting is performed and the auditors begin the planning phase of the audit, the PBC List must be sent out to the client. An initial PBC List would be to request specific walkthrough meetings to address various Test of Design (TOD) audit procedures, such as inquiring of management to gain an understanding of the change-management process or how users authenticate to various applications and so on.

The initial PBC List would also involve requesting any sort of policies and procedures as they relate to the various control families (Access Controls, Configuration Management, Segregation of Duties and the like). Each PBC item should contain a PBC number, brief description of the item being requested, the purpose of the request, the requested date, the due date, and status (open, closed, partial, overdue). The due date will be negotiated in the contract and is usually 3-5 business days for most PBC requests; however, it can be shorter or longer, depending on the SOW or contract negotiated.

As PBC items are provided by the client to the auditor, the auditor will then make a determination of whether the PBC item is sufficient or not sufficient and why. Below is a listing of common columns that should be included in a PBC List:

PBC Number	Type of Request	Item Description	Requested by	Date Requested	Due Date	Auditor Comments

It is important to note that when you reach a point during the Test of Effectiveness (TOE) phase, where you need to request a population of users or changes for testing, sufficient verification and validation of populations is carried out prior to selecting a sample. In a contractor role supporting an Inspector General or the GAO, for example, they will ask the auditor how he or she gained assurance that the population received by the client is complete and accurate. For example, if you wanted to obtain a population of users from System X, you will first need to submit a PBC request to the effect of:

> "We would like to observe and obtain a system generated listing/ population of users that have access to System X. Data elements such as Full Name, User Name, Role/Function, Last Login Date, and Account Creation Date are being requested as part of this data pull."

Before meeting with the individual who will be pulling these users for you, first analyze the script or query being used within the application to ensure that it is sufficient. If you don't have the technical expertise to review this script, at least obtain it so that you can have a member of your technical team review it at a later time. When the population of users is generated in front of your eyes, AKA an observation by you, the auditor, then the process owner should take a screenshot of the top of the list and the bottom of the list so that you can verify the total population of users, as well as the first couple and the last couple of users.

Make sure the process owner sends you an email of these screenshots before you leave the meeting so that you will be able to verify that the information you receive after the meeting is consistent with what you observed during the data pull. This will prove to your client (i.e. IG or GAO and so on) that you have performed a sufficient level of validation to ensure a complete and accurate population of users. Remember when pulling any sort of population that a system-generated listing is always going to be the best form of data extraction, since there is minimal room for data manipulation by the auditee.

Below is an example of a PBC List:

K2 IT//Audit//Security		**PBC List**					
Request #	FISCAM Control Category	Description	Date Requested	Due Date	Status (Open, Closed, Partial)	XXX Agency/Client POC name that provided this PBC request.	Comments
1	Security Management (SM)	Entity-level information security Standard Operating Procedure (SOP) that details the various information security requirements applicable to all systems/devices on XXX Agency/Client networks.	10/20/2019	Date set forth in Contract. If PBC requests have a turnaround time of 10 days, add 10 days to the request date.	Update this column to Open, Closed, or Partial based on the items delivered.	Use this column to be able to ask clarifying questions if a PBC item that was delivered is not clear or raises questions. This way, you target your questions to the person that delivered the request and has first hand knowledge of what they provided and why they provided it to satisfy the PBC request.	Use this column to make notes about the history of this request. In the event that the PBC documentation delivered only partially satisfies the request, you can note this in the "Comments" column and note exactly what is missing when you send the updated PBC List back to the XXX Agency/Client.
2	Security Management (SM)	Proposed FIPS 199 security categorization of XXX System information system (Low, Moderate, High)					
3	Configuration Management (CM)	XXX System configuration management plan and associated policies around: 1. Change-management process (how changes are tracked, requested, authorized, and tested prior to being deployed to production) 2. Vulnerability scanning process 3. Server baseline configuration 4. Scanning and checklist deployment 5. Emergency change process 6. Patch management process					

4	Access Controls (AC)	XXX System user access control policies and procedures around: 1. User authentication 2. User provisioning and deprovisioning (terminations) 3. Access recertifications 4. Audit logging and monitoring 5. Incident response 6. Password parameters					
5	Security Management (SM)	Please provide the Authority to Operate (ATO) package for the XXXX System, which includes the following documentation: 1. System Security Plan (SSP) 2. ATO letter 3. Security Assessment Report (SAR) 4. POA&Ms					

It is important to note that a proper PBC request should be surgical, noninvasive, and fully descriptive of what the auditor is looking for from the audit client in order to minimize any follow up after the PBC has been submitted. Overall audit progress can be impacted severely if the auditor fails to document PBC requests in a clear and concise manner.

After the initial PBC request list has been submitted, planning the scope of our audit can begin. This involves the creation of an Audit Work Program or AWP. The AWP is essentially the work plan for the audit, and it documents all of the controls that will be tested as well as their testing procedures. The Test of Design (TOD) and Test of Effectiveness (TOE) procedures should both be included in this AWP. Now, with respect to planning an audit and developing an AWP, the IT auditor needs to understand that not all FISCAM controls can be tested in one year or testing period. Thus, the auditor must carefully select the most important controls to test for each system based on risk.

Additionally, when developing the AWP, the auditor must understand that some controls can be combined with other controls, as they are similar and are all part of a single process. Let's take configuration management for example. Controls CM-3.1–3.5 are usually combined because they involve analyzing the change-management process and how changes are appropriately documented/tracked, requested, authorized, tested, and approved prior to being deployed to the production environment. After selecting all of the controls for testing, schedule walkthrough meetings with the key process owners at the agency being audited.

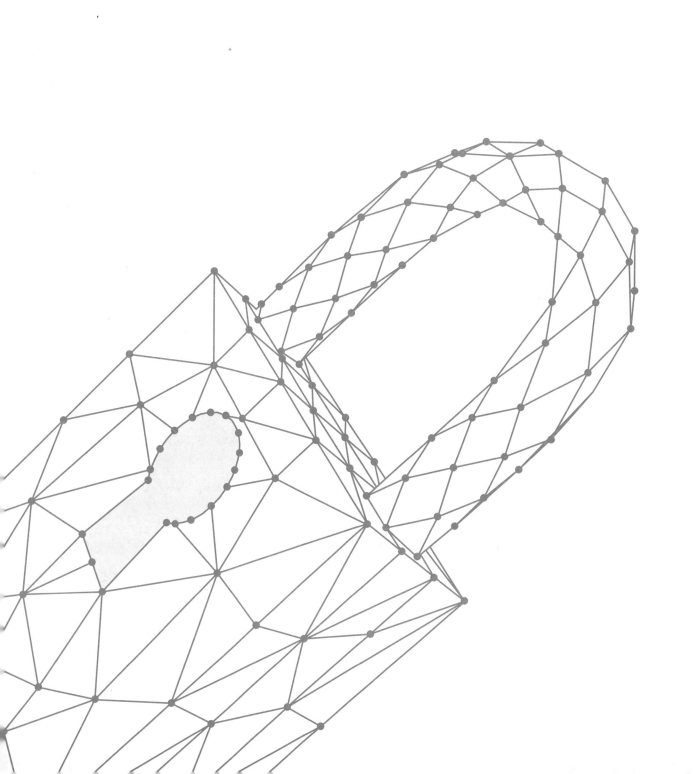

CHAPTER 8
THE IT AUDIT PROCESS IN PRACTICE

• •

Think back to Chapter 3 where we uncovered all the steps, conceptually speaking, of how to initiate and conduct an audit. But what does that look like in practice? Let us examine the pragmatic steps an auditor will take to initiate and conduct fieldwork.

The IT audit process begins with the identification of the customer. Let's assume we are a federal contractor that has been awarded a prime contract to perform a FISCAM audit of an agency. After all the contractual procedures have been performed, we begin with a kick-off meeting with the agency being audited to describe the "what, where, when, why, and how":

- Why we are there in the first place. We are contracted by the Office of the Inspector General or the Government Accountability Office, for example, to perform an audit of the information systems supporting the financial statements of the agency.

- What we are auditing. What systems? What is the scope?

- Where we will be performing the work.

- When we will be performing the work and our proposed timeline.

- How we will be performing the work.

Planning Phase

We will now go into detail about how we will be performing this audit.

The process begins with the "planning phase," whereby we submit a Provided by Client (PBC) List. This is a list of all the initial supporting documentation we need to request from the agency in order to gain a better understanding of what types of controls are in place and the IT policies and procedures that are being followed to satisfy those control objectives. These PBC requests usually require us to give the agency a few days (usually 5-7 business days) to fulfill the PBC requests. PBC requests will usually be in the form of an Excel spreadsheet.

After the initial PBC request list has been submitted, we then begin planning the scope of our audit. This involves the creation of an Audit Work Program or AWP. The AWP is essentially the work plan for the audit that documents all of the controls that will be tested as well as their testing procedures. The Test of Design (TOD) and Test of Operating Effectiveness (TOE) procedures should both be included in this AWP.

Now, with respect to planning an audit and developing an AWP, the IT auditor needs to understand that not all FISCAM controls can be tested in one year or testing period. Thus, the IT auditor must carefully select the most important controls to test for each system based on risk. Additionally, when developing the AWP, the IT auditor must understand that some controls can be combined with other controls, as they are similar and all part of a single process. Let's take configuration management for example. Controls CM-3.1–3.5 are usually combined because they involve analyzing the change-management process and how changes are appropriately documented/tracked, requested, authorized, tested, and approved prior to being deployed to the production environment. After we have selected all of the controls we will be testing, we then schedule walkthrough meetings with the key process owners at the agency we are auditing.

TOD Phase

We now enter the Test of Design (TOD) phase of the audit. The purpose of these walkthroughs is to gain a better understanding of the control environment and documented our inquiry. The key part of TOD involves inquiring with management and inspecting key policy/procedure documentation to validate that the process we inquired about is documented accurately and is consistent. After we document our inquiry, we should also be receiving our policy/procedure documentation from the initial PBC List that we submitted a few days ago. Now we need to assess these documents based on our testing procedures in the AWP and document our results in our workpapers.

For example, when testing changes, the TOD phase would involve:

- Performing inquiry with management to understand the change process and how changes are made to a system at all layers (OS, DB, APP).

- Requesting the change management/configuration management plan to determine if it contains all necessary elements per NIST requirements and is consistent with the inquiry performed.

TOE Phase

The Test of Effectiveness (TOE) phase involves selecting samples for testing, obtaining screenshots of configuration settings, and determining whether the control is actually operating effectively. Samples are selected in the following control areas:

- Access controls. When performing new-user testing (sample of new users)

- Audit logging. (Sample of audit logs)

- Access recertifications. (Selecting a sample of access recertifications for privileged users and end users)

- Termination testing. (100 percent of terminations should be tested as a best practice; 100 percent of inactive users should be tested as a best practice)

- Configuration management. When testing changes, vulnerability scanning. (Sample of vulnerability scans selected)

For example, when testing changes, the TOE phase would involve:

- Obtaining a population of all changes made to a system.

- Selecting a sample of those changes based on an approved sampling methodology.

- Requesting all change documentation including change request forms, approvals, evidence of test plans/testing, and performing an evaluation to determine if the change management process was followed appropriately.

CHAPTER 9

SAMPLE AUDIT WORK PROGRAMS FOR PERFORMING FISCAM ASSESSMENTS

• •

The Audit Work Program or (AWP) is essentially your audit plan with respect to the controls you plan to test and the associated TOD and TOE procedures. The AWP is developed during the planning stages of every audit. The FISCAM manual will help tremendously when trying to develop your AWP, as it contains all the relevant control categories such as AC, CM, SM, IN, DA, BP, SD, CP, as well as the critical elements, control activities, and control techniques. Testing procedures are defined at the control technique level in FISCAM. Thus, after you have defined the critical elements within each control category that you would like to test, you will then select the applicable control activities and control techniques. When developing the audit work program, the auditor is warranted a level of flexibility with respect to combining various control techniques and developing "buckets" within each control family, which will then translate into individual workpapers. For example, below is a listing of some important FISCAM controls which are separated by IT general controls and application level controls. Within FISCAM, any controls starting with "AS-xx" are application level controls. Thus, an ITGC control in access controls will start with "AC-xx," while an application control within access controls will start with "AS-xx." Below is a listing of some major controls within access controls, configuration management, segregation of duties, and other control families, which have been combined and separated by colors to express a possible workpaper combination.

ACCESS CONTROLS (AC) – AUDIT WORK PROGRAM CONTROL COMBINATIONS

NOTE: *The list below shows that you can combine control techniques when developing an audit work program. Another concept we would like to express in the list is how FISCAM breaks down ITGC-level access controls (delineated by "AC-x.x.x") vs. application level access controls (delineated by "AS-x.x.x"). You will also notice that the corresponding application control descriptions are similar, if not identical, to the ITGC control descriptions they have been matched with below.*

ITGC Control Number (AC)	Control Description	Application Control Number (AS)	Control Description
AC-1.1.1.	Connectivity, including access paths and control technologies between systems and to internal system resources, is documented, approved by appropriate entity management, and consistent with risk.	AS-2.1.1	Application boundaries are identified in security plans. Application boundaries are adequately secure.
AC-1.1.2.	Networks are appropriately configured to adequately protect access paths within and between systems, using appropriate technological controls (e.g. routers, firewalls, etc.)		

AC-1.2.1.	The information system prevents further access to the system by initiating a session lock after a specified period of inactivity that remains in effect until the user reestablishes access using identification and authentication procedures.	**AS-2.3.2**	The application locks the user's account after a predetermined number of attempts to log on with an invalid password. The application may automatically reset the user account after a specific time period (an hour or a day), or may require an administrator to reset the account.
AC-1.2.2	Where connectivity is not continual, network connection automatically disconnects at the end of a session.		If the user is away from his/her workspace for a preset amount of time or if the user's session is inactive, the application automatically logs off the user's account.
AC-2.1.7.	Attempts to log on with invalid passwords are limited (e.g., 3–7 attempts).	**AS-2.3.4**	Multiple log-ons are controlled and monitored.
AC-2.1.14.	Concurrent sessions are appropriately controlled.		

The combination of these controls could be in one workpaper within Access Controls. Thus, you can cover OS, DB using the AC controls and Application layer using the respecting AS control.

AC-2.1.1.	Identification and authentication is unique to each user (or processes acting on behalf of users), except in specially approved instances (for example, public websites or other publicly available information systems).	**AS-2.2.1**	Identification and authentication is unique to each user. Application boundaries are adequately secure.
		AS-2.3.3	Each application user has only one user ID.
AC-2.1.2.	Account policies (including authentication policies and lockout policies) are appropriate given the risk, and enforced.	**AS-2.3.1**	The entity has formal procedures and processes for granting users access to the application. The entity's IT security policies and procedures contain guidance for: • Assigning passwords; • Changing and resetting passwords; and • Handling lost or compromised passwords.
AC-2.1.3.	Effective procedures are implemented to determine compliance with identification and authentication policies.		

		AS-2.5.1	The entity implements a security plan and process for 1) identification and authorization of users; 2) access controls for limited user privileges; 3) use of digital signatures; 4) prohibition of direct access by the public to production data; and 5) compliance with NIST guidance.
AC-2.1.4.	Selection of authentication methods (for example, passwords, tokens, biometrics, key cards, PKI certificates, or a combination therein) are appropriate, based on risk.		
AC-2.1.5.	Authenticators: • are adequately controlled by the assigned user and not subject to disclosure; and • cannot be easily guessed or duplicated. Additional considerations for passwords are described below.		
AC-2.1.12.	Use of and access to authenticators is controlled (e.g., their use is not shared with other users).		
AC-2.1.13.	Effective procedures are implemented to handle lost, compromised, or damaged authenticators (e.g., tokens, PKI certificates, biometrics, passwords, and key cards).		

AC-2.1.6.	Password-based authenticators: • are not displayed when entered; • are changed periodically (e.g., every 30 to 90 days); • contain alphanumeric and special characters; • are sufficiently long (e.g., at least 8 characters in length); • have an appropriate life (automatically expire); • are prohibited from reuse for a specified period of time (e.g., at least 6 generations); and • are not the same as the user ID.		
AC-2.1.7.	Authentication information is obscured (e.g., password is not displayed).		
AC-2.1.8.	Use of easily guessed passwords (such as names or words) are prohibited.		
AC-2.1.9.	Generic user IDs and passwords are not used.		
AC-2.1.10.	Vendor-supplied default passwords are replaced during installation.		
AC-2.1.11.	Passwords embedded in programs are prohibited. (Note: An embedded password is a password that is included into the source code of an application or utility. Applications often need to communicate with other applications and systems and this requires an "authentication" process that is sometimes accomplished through the use of embedded passwords).		

AC-2.1.15.	Where appropriate, digital signatures, PKI, and electronic signatures are effectively implemented.		
AC-2.1.16.	PKI-based authentication: • validates certificates by constructing a certification path to an accepted trust anchor; • establishes user control of the corresponding private key; and • maps the authenticated identity to the user account.		
AC-3.1.1.	Resource owners have identified authorized users and the access they are authorized to have.	**AS-2.4.1**	Before a user obtains a user account and password for the application, the user's level of access has been authorized by a manager and the application administrator.
AC-3.1.2.	Security administration personnel set parameters of security software to provide access as authorized and restrict access that has not been authorized. This includes access to data files, load and source code libraries (if applicable), security files, and operating system files. Standard naming conventions are established and used effectively as a basis for controlling access to data and programs. (Standard naming conventions are essential to ensure effective configuration management identification and control of production files and programs vs. test files and programs.)		

For groupings of controls that do not have a respective AS level control, you can still test this control at the application layer within the workpaper if it is applicable to that specific application/system.

AC-3.1.3.	Security managers review access authorizations and discuss any questionable authorizations with resource owners.	**AS-2.6.3**	Security administrators review application user access authorizations for access to sensitive transactions and discuss any questionable authorizations with owners.
AC-3.1.4.	All changes to security access authorizations are automatically logged and periodically reviewed by management independent of the security function; unusual activity is investigated.		
AC-3.1.5.	Resource owners periodically review access authorizations for continuing appropriateness.	**AS-2.4.2**	Owners periodically review access to ensure continued appropriateness.
AC-3.1.6.	Access is limited to individuals with a valid business purpose (least privilege).	**AS-2.4.3**	Access is limited to individuals with a valid business purpose (least privilege).
AC-3.1.7.	Unnecessary accounts (default, guest accounts) are removed, disabled, or otherwise secured.		
AC-3.1.8.	Inactive accounts and accounts for terminated individuals are disabled or removed in a timely manner.	**AS-2.6.5**	Inactive accounts and accounts for terminated individuals are disabled or removed in a timely manner.
AC-3.1.9.	Access to shared file systems are restricted to the extent possible (for example, only to particular hosts, and only for the level of access required).		
AC-3.1.10.	Emergency or temporary access (e.g., firewall IDs) is appropriately controlled: • Documented and maintained • Approved by appropriate managers • Securely communicated to the security function		

	• Automatically terminated after a predetermined period • All activity is logged		
AC-4.1.1.	Access to sensitive/privileged accounts is restricted to individuals or processes having a legitimate need for the purposes of accomplishing a valid business purpose.	**AS-2.6.6**	Access to sensitive transactions is limited to individuals with a valid business purpose (least privilege).
		AS-2.6.2	Owners authorize users to have access to sensitive transactions or activities.
AC-4.1.2.	Use of sensitive/privileged accounts is adequately monitored.	**AS-2.6.4**	Owners periodically review access to sensitive transactions and activities to ensure continued appropriateness.
		AS-2.6.1	Owners have identified sensitive transactions or activities for the business process.
AC-4.3.1.	Cryptographic tools have been implemented to protect the integrity and confidentiality of sensitive and critical data and software programs where appropriate.		
AC-4.3.2.	Encryption procedures are implemented in data communications where appropriate based on risk.		
AC-4.3.3.	For authentication to a cryptographic module, the information system employs appropriate authentication methods.		
AC-4.3.4.	The information system employs automated mechanisms with supporting procedures or manual procedures for cryptographic key establishment and key management.		

AC-5.1.1.	An effective incident-response program has been implemented and includes: • Documented policies, procedures, and plans • Documented testing of the incident response plan and follow-up on findings • A means of prompt centralized reporting • Active monitoring of alerts/advisories • Response team members with the necessary knowledge, skills, and abilities • Training on roles and responsibilities and periodic refresher training • Links to other relevant groups • Protection against denial-of-service attacks (see http://icat.nist.gov) • Appropriate incident-response assistance • Consideration of computer forensics		
AC-5.2.1.	An effective intrusion detection system has been implemented, including appropriate placement of intrusion-detection sensors and incident thresholds.		
AC-5.2.2.	An effective process has been established based on a risk assessment, to identify auditable events that will be logged.	**AS-2.8.1**	Policies and procedures are established to reasonably assure that application security audit and monitoring is effective.

AC-5.2.3.	All auditable events, including access to and modifications of sensitive or critical system resources, are logged.	AS-2.9.1	Logging and other parameters are appropriately set up to notify of security violations as they occur.
AC-5.2.4.	Audit records contain appropriate information for effective review including sufficient information to establish what events occurred, when the events occurred (for example, time stamps), the source of the events, and the outcome of the events.		
AC-5.2.5.	Audit record storage capacity is adequate and configured to prevent such capacity from being exceeded. In the event of an audit failure or audit storage capacity being reached, the information system alerts officials and appropriate action is taken.		
AC-5.2.6.	Audit records and tools are protected from unauthorized access, modification, and deletion. Audit records are effectively reviewed for unusual or suspicious activity or violations.		
AC-5.2.7.	Audit records are retained long enough to provide support for after-the-fact investigations of security incidents and to meet regulatory and organizational information retention requirements.		
AC-5.3.1.	Security violations and activities, including failed logon attempts, other failed access attempts, and sensitive activity, are reported and investigated.	AS-2.10.1	Reportable exceptions and violations are identified and logged. Exception reports are generated and reviewed by security administration. If an exception occurs, specific action is taken based upon the nature of exception.

AC-5.3.2.	Security managers investigate security to violations and suspicious activities and report results to appropriate supervisory and management personnel.		
AC-5.3.3.	Appropriate disciplinary actions are taken.		
AC-5.3.4.	Violations and incidents are analyzed, summarized, and reported to senior management and appropriate government authorities.		
AC-6.1.1.	Use a risk management approach to identify the level of physical security needed for the facility and implement measures commensurate with the risks of physical damage or access.	**AS-2.11.1**	Physical controls are integrated with entity-wide and system-level controls. Application resources sensitive to physical access are identified and appropriate physical security is placed over them.
AC-6.1.2.	Facilities and areas housing sensitive and critical resources have been identified. The following generally constitute sensitive areas: computer rooms, tape libraries, telecommunication closets, mechanical/ electrical rooms, cooling facilities, and data transmission and power lines.	**AS-2.7.1**	The entity identifies sensitive application resources. Access to sensitive application resources is restricted to appropriate users. Sensitive application data is encrypted, where appropriate.
AC-6.1.3.	All significant threats to the physical wellbeing of these resources have been identified and related risks determined.		
AC-6.1.5.	Conduct annual employee physical security awareness training. Coordinate this step with SM-4.		

CONFIGURATION MANAGEMENT (CM) – AUDIT WORK PROGRAM CONTROLS

NOTE: *Expressed in the below listing of CM and corresponding AS level controls within configuration management is the concept of adjusting the AWP to remove any redundant controls and various justifications for not including certain FISCAM controls into the audit scope. FISCAM contains many redundant controls and, thus, as long as you can justify why you are not including a certain control into the testing, you can provide the client (e.g., Inspector General or a DOD agency or the Government Accountability Office) assurance that you, as the external auditor, have done the due diligence to develop a sufficient AWP.*

ITGC Control Number	Control Description	Application Control Number (AS)	Control Description	Scope In/ Out	Sample Justification to Scope OUT this control Technique
CM-1.1.1.	An effective configuration management process is documented and implemented, including: • A CM plan that identifies roles, responsibilities, procedures, and documentation requirements • Guidance that is appropriate for personnel with varying levels of skill and experience • Trained personnel who are familiar with the organization's configuration management process • Permitting only essential capabilities and restricting the use of dangerous functions, ports, protocols, and services • Regular review and approval of configuration changes by management; for example, Configuration Control Board (CCB) • Appropriate representation on CCB from across the entity	**AS-3.3.1**	A SDLC methodology has been developed that • provides a structured approach consistent with generally accepted concepts and practices, including active user involvement throughout the process; • is sufficiently documented to provide guidance to staff with varying levels of skill and experience; • provides a means of controlling changes in requirements that occur over the system life; and • includes documentation requirements.	In	N/A

	• A formal SDLC methodology that includes system-level security engineering principles to be considered in the design, development, and operation of an information system • Appropriate systems documentation				
CM-2.1.1.	A current and comprehensive baseline inventory of hardware, software, and firmware is documented, backed up, and protected.			In	N/A
CM-2.1.2.	Hardware, software, and firmware are mapped to application it supports.			In	N/A
CM-2.1.3.	Configuration settings optimize the system's security features.			In	N/A
CM-3.1.1.	An appropriate formal change management process is documented.	**AS-3.1.1**	Appropriate policies and procedures are established for application configuration management.	In	N/A
CM-3.1.2.	Configuration changes are authorized by management. Configuration management actions are recorded in sufficient detail so that the content and status of each configuration item is known and previous versions can be recovered.	**AS-3.4.1**	Change request forms are used to document requests and related projects.	In	N/A
CM-3.1.3.	Relevant stakeholders have access to and knowledge of the configuration status of the configuration items.	**AS-3.4.2**	Change requests must be approved by both system users and IT staff.	Out	We are testing that change requests must be authorized and approved prior to being deployed to production in CM-3.1.12 and AS-3.5.8. This control is redundant.

CM-3.1.4.	Detailed specifications are prepared by the programmer and reviewed by a programming supervisor for system and application software changes.	AS-3.5.2	Detailed system specifications are prepared by the programmer and reviewed by a programming supervisor.	Out	We are testing to verify that system integration and system acceptance testing are being conducted in CM-3.1.8. This control is redundant.
CM-3.1.5.	Test plan standards have been developed for all levels of testing that define responsibilities for each party (for example, users, system analysts, programmers, auditors, quality assurance, library control).	AS-3.5.1	Test plan standards have been developed for all levels of testing that define responsibilities for each party (e.g., users, system analysis, programmers, auditors, quality assurance, library control).	In	N/A
CM-3.1.6.	Test plans are documented and approved that define responsibilities for each party involved (for example, users, systems analysts, programmers, auditors, quality assurance, library control).	AS-3.5.4	Test plans are documented and approved that define responsibilities for each party involved.	In	N/A
CM-3.1.7.	Test plans include appropriate consideration of security.			In	N/A
CM-3.1.8.	Unit, integration, and system testing are performed and approved in accordance with the test plan and apply a sufficient range of valid and invalid conditions.	AS-3.5.5	Unit, integration, and system testing are performed and approved in accordance with the test plan and applying a sufficient range of valid and invalid conditions.	In	N/A
CM-3.1.9.	A comprehensive set of test transactions and data is developed that represents the various activities and conditions that will be encountered in processing.	AS-3.5.6	A comprehensive set of test transactions and data is developed that represents the various activities and conditions that will be encountered in processing.	In	N/A

CM-3.1.10.	Live data are not used in testing of program changes except to build test data files.			In	N/A
CM-3.1.11.	Test results are documented and appropriate responsive actions are taken based on the results.	AS-3.5.7	Test results are reviewed and documented.	In	N/A
CM-3.1.12.	Program changes are moved into production only when approved by management and by persons independent of the programmer.	AS-3.5.8	Program changes are moved into production only upon documented approval from users and system development management.	In	N/A
CM-3.1.16.	Program development and maintenance, testing, and production programs are maintained separately (for example, libraries) and movement between these areas is appropriately controlled, including appropriate consideration of segregation of duties (see the Segregation of Duties control category).	AS-3.6.1	Separate libraries are maintained for program development and maintenance, testing, and production programs.	In	N/A
		AS-3.6.2	Source code is maintained in a separate library.	In	N/A
		AS-3.7.1	A group independent of the user programmers control movement of programs and data among libraries.	Out	This control is covered in CM-3.1.12 and thus is redundant.
CM-3.1.17.	Access to all programs, including production code, source code, and extra program copies, are adequately protected.	AS-3.6.3	Access to all programs, including production code, source code, and extra program copies are protected by access control software and operating system features.	In	N/A
CM-3.1.18.	Configuration changes to network devices (for example, routers and firewalls) are properly controlled and documented.			Out	This control will be reviewed at the MCEN-N level as these controls are performed by MCOG. MCOG manages authentication to network devices such as

					firewalls and routers for the perimeter of the primary domain (MCEN-N). Thus, MCOG provides perimeter security for the various enclaves where our in-scope systems reside.
CM-4.1.1.	Routinely validate that the current configuration information is accurate, up-to-date, and working as intended for networks, operating systems, and infrastructure applications.	**AS-3.2.1**	The entity maintains information on the current configuration of the application.	In	N/A
CM-4.1.2.	The verification and validation criteria for the configuration audit is appropriate and specifies how the configuration item will be evaluated in terms of correctness, consistency, necessity, completeness, and performance.			In	N/A
CM-4.1.4.	The information system periodically verifies the correct operation of security functions on system start up and restart, on command by user with appropriate privilege (providing system audit trail documentation) and takes appropriate action (for example, notifies system administrator, shuts the system down, restarts the system) when anomalies are discovered.			In	N/A
CM-5.1.1.	Information systems are scanned periodically to detect known vulnerabilities.	**AS-3.13.1**	The entity follows an effective process to identify vulnerabilities in applications and update them.	Out	**We are assessing vulnerabilities at the OS and DB layers.**
CM-5.1.2.	An effective patch management process is documented and implemented, including: • Identification of systems affected by recently announced software vulnerabilities			In	N/A

	• Prioritization of patches based on system configuration and risk • Appropriate installation of patches on a timely basis, including testing for effectiveness and potential side effects on the entity's systems • Verification that patches, service packs, and hotfixes were appropriately installed on affected systems				
CM-5.1.3.	Software is up-to-date; the latest versions of software patches are installed.			In	N/A
CM-5.1.4.	An effective virus, spam, and spyware protection process is documented and implemented, including: • Appropriate policies and procedures • Effective protection software is installed that identifies and isolates suspected viruses, spam, and spyware • Virus, spam, and spyware definitions are up-to-date			In	N/A
CM-6.1.1.	Appropriately document and implement procedures for emergency changes.			In	N/A
CM-6.2.1.	Appropriately document and approve emergency changes to the configuration and notify appropriate personnel for analysis and follow-up.	**AS-3.14.1**	The entity follows an effective process to properly document, test, and approve emergency changes.	In	N/A
N/A	This application control does not have a corresponding CM control. However, it may be covered in a BP, IN, or DA control and thus can be integrated there.	**AS-3.8.1**	User accounts are assigned to a role in the application. Roles are designed and approved by management to provide appropriate access and prevent an unauthorized user from executing critical transactions in production that	Out	This testing will be conducted/ satisfied during BP testing as all INPUTs into the application are reviewed to ensure access is restricted for sensitive transactions.

			change application functionality.		Testing of access controls for privileged users also provides coverage for this control.
N/A	This application control does not have a corresponding CM control. However, it may be covered in a BP, IN, or DA control and thus can be integrated there.	**AS-3.9.1**	Changes to application programs, codes, and tables are either restricted or denied in the production environment. All changes are made using the approved change control process. User access to the application programs, codes, and tables is provided only for emergency user IDs.	Out	We are already covering access to source code and production environment in CM-3.1.17
N/A	This application control does not have a corresponding CM control. However, it may be covered in a BP, IN, or DA control and thus can be integrated there.	**AS-3.10.1**	Security design includes consideration for sensitive administration (system) transactions and restricted user access to these transactions.	Out	This testing will be conducted/satisfied during BP testing as all INPUTs into the application are reviewed to ensure access is restricted for sensitive transactions. Testing of access controls for privileged users also provides coverage for this control.
N/A	This application control does not have a corresponding CM control. However, it may be covered in a BP, IN, or DA control and thus can be integrated there.	**AS-3.11.1**	Procedures are established to reasonably assure that key program and table changes are monitored by a responsible individual who does not have the change authority. The procedures provide the details of reports/logs to run, specific valuation criteria and frequency of, assessment.	Out	This testing will be conducted/satisfied during BP testing as all INPUTs into the application are reviewed to ensure access is restricted for sensitive transactions. Also, there are various auditing and logging controls within Access Controls that should cover this. AC-2.9.1, AC-2.10.1

CONTINGENCY PLANNING (CP) – AUDIT WORK PROGRAM CONTROLS

ITGC Control Number (CP)	Control Description	Application Control Number (AS)	Control Description
CP-1.1.1.	The entity categorizes information systems in accordance with appropriate guidance, such as FIPS 199, and documents the results in the system security plan.		
CP-3.1.1.	A contingency plan has been documented that • is based on clearly defined contingency planning policy; • reflects current conditions, including system interdependencies; • has been approved by key affected groups, including senior management, information security and data center management, and program managers; • clearly assigns responsibilities for recovery; • includes detailed instructions for restoring operations (both operating system and critical applications); • identifies the alternate processing facility and the back up storage facility; • includes procedures to follow when the data/service center is unable to receive or transmit data; • identifies critical data files; • is detailed enough to be understood by all entity managers;	**AS-5.3.1** **AS-5.3.2**	Develop a time-based application contingency plan. Incorporate the application contingency plan into related plans, such as the disaster recovery, business continuity, and business resumption plans.

	• includes computer and telecommunications hardware compatible with the entity's needs; • includes necessary contact numbers; • includes appropriate system-recovery instructions; • has been distributed to all appropriate personnel; and • has been coordinated with related plans and activities.		
CP-1.1.2	A list of critical operations and data has been documented that • identifies primary mission or business functions; • prioritizes data and operations; • is approved by senior program managers; and • reflects current conditions including system interdependencies and technologies.	**AS-5.1.1**	Determine the critical functions performed by the application and identify the IT resources, including key data and programs required to perform them.
CP-1.2.1.	Resources supporting critical operations and functions have been identified and documented. Types of resources identified should include the following: • Computer hardware • Computer software • Computer supplies • Network components • System documentation • Telecommunications • Office facilities and supplies • Human resources		
CP-2.1.4.	The information system backup and recovery procedures adequately provide for recovery and reconstitution to the system's original state after a disruption or failure including the following:		

	• system parameters are reset; • patches are reinstalled; • configuration settings are reestablished; • system documentation and operating procedures are available; • application and system software is reinstalled; • information from the most recent backup is available; and • the system is fully tested.		
CP-3.1.5.	User departments have developed adequate manual/peripheral processing procedures for use until operations are restored.		
CP-3.1.3.	Procedures allow facility access in support of restoration of lost information under the contingency plans in the event of an emergency.		
CP-3.1.4.	The plan provides for backup personnel so that it can be implemented independent of specific individuals.		
CP-2.4.1.	Policies and procedures exist and are up to date.		
CP-1.2.2.	Critical information technology resources have been analyzed to determine their impact on operations if a given resource were disrupted or damaged. This analysis should evaluate the impact of the outages over time and across related resources and dependent systems.	**AS-5.1.2**	Identify the disruption impacts and allowable outage times for the application.
CP-1.3.1.	Emergency processing priorities have been are documented and approved by appropriate program and data processing managers.	**AS-5.1.3**	Develop recovery priorities that will help determine recovery strategies.

CP-2.1.1.	Backup files are created on a prescribed basis and rotated off-site often enough to avoid disruption if current files are lost or damaged.	**AS-5.2.1**	Backup files of key application data are created on a prescribed basis.
CP-2.1.2.	System and application documentation is maintained at the off-site storage location.	**AS-5.2.2**	Current application programs are copied and available for use.
CP-2.1.3.	The backup storage site is geographically removed from the primary site (for example, not subject to the same hazards) and protected by environmental controls and physical access controls.	**AS-5.2.3**	Backup files of application data and programs are securely stored off-site and retrievable for contingency plan implementation.
CP-3.1.6.	Several copies of the current contingency plan are securely stored off-site at different locations.		
CP-2.2.1.	Fire detection and suppression devices have been installed and are working; for example, smoke detectors, fire extinguishers, and sprinkler systems.		
CP-2.2.2.	Controls have been implemented to mitigate other disasters, such as floods, earthquakes, terrorism, etc.		
CP-2.2.3.	Redundancy exists in critical systems (for example, power and air-cooling systems).		
CP-2.2.4.	Building plumbing lines do not endanger the computer facility or, at a minimum, shut-off valves and procedures exist and are known.		
CP-2.2.5.	An uninterruptible power supply or backup generator has been provided so that power will be adequate for orderly shut down.		

CP-2.2.6.	Humidity, temperature, and voltage are controlled within acceptable levels.		
CP-2.2.7.	Emergency lighting activates in the event of a power outage and covers emergency exits and evacuation routes.		
CP-2.2.8.	A master power switch or emergency shut-off switch is present and appropriately located.		
CP-2.2.9.	Environmental controls are periodically tested at least annually for federal agencies.		
CP-2.2.10.	Eating, drinking, and other behavior that may damage computer equipment is prohibited.		
CP-2.3.1.	Operational and support personnel have received training and understand their emergency roles and responsibilities.		
CP-2.3.2.	Personnel receive periodic environmental controls training including emergency fire, water, and alarm incident procedures.		
CP-2.4.3.	Regular and unscheduled maintenance performed is documented.		
CP-2.4.2.	Routine periodic hardware preventive maintenance is scheduled and performed in accordance with vendor specifications and in a manner that minimizes the impact on operations.		
CP-2.4.5.	Spare or backup hardware is used to provide a high level of system availability for critical and sensitive applications.		
CP-3.2.2.	Alternate network and telecommunication services have been arranged.		

CP-2.3.3.	Emergency response procedures are documented.		
CP-2.3.4.	Emergency procedures are periodically tested.		
CP-2.4.4.	Flexibility exists in the data processing operations to accommodate regular and a reasonable amount of unscheduled maintenance.		
CP-2.4.6.	Goals are established by senior management on the availability of data processing and online services.		
CP-2.4.7.	Records are maintained on the actual performance in meeting service schedules.		
CP-2.4.8.	Problems and delays encountered, the reason and the elapsed time for resolution are recorded and analyzed to identify recurring patterns or trends.		
CP-2.4.9.	Senior management periodically reviews and compares the service performance achieved with the goals and surveys of user departments to see if their needs are being met.		
CP-2.4.10.	Changes of hardware equipment and related software are scheduled to minimize the impact on operations and users, thus allowing for adequate testing.		
CP-2.4.11.	Advance notification of hardware changes and related software changes is given to users so that service is not unexpectedly interrupted.		

CP-3.1.2.	Contingency plans are reevaluated before proposed changes to the information system are approved to determine if major modifications have security ramifications that require operational changes in order to maintain adequate risk mitigation.		
CP-3.1.7.	The contingency plan is periodically reassessed and revised as appropriate. At a minimum, the plan is reassessed when there are significant changes in the entity mission, organization, business processes, and IT infrastructures (e.g. hardware, software, personnel).		
CP-3.2.1.	Contracts or inter-entity agreements have been established for backup processing facilities that • are in a state of readiness commensurate with the risks of interrupted operations; • have sufficient processing and storage capacity; and • are likely to be available for use.		
CP-3.2.3.	Arrangements are planned for travel, lodging, and protection of necessary personnel, if needed.		
CP-4.1.1.	The contingency plan is periodically tested under conditions that simulate a disaster. Disaster scenarios tested may be rotated periodically. Typically, contingency plans are tested annually or as soon as possible after a significant change to the environment that would alter the assessed risk.	**AS-5.4.1**	The application contingency plan is periodically tested and test conditions include disaster simulations.
		AS-5.4.2	The following areas are included in the contingency test: • System recovery on an alternate platform from backup media

			• Coordination among recovery teams • Internal and external connectivity • System performance using alternate equipment • Restoration of normal operations • Notification procedures
CP-4.2.1.	Test results are documented, and a report, such as a lessons-learned report, is developed and provided to senior management.	**AS-5.4.3**	Test results are documented and a report, such as a lessons-learned report, is developed and provided to senior management.
CP-4.2.2.	The contingency plan and related agreements and preparations are adjusted to correct any deficiencies identified during testing.	**AS-5.4.4**	The contingency plan and related agreements and preparations are adjusted to correct any deficiencies identified during testing.
		AS-5.3.3	Contingency operations provide for an effective control environment by restricting and monitoring user access to application data and programs: • Users are identified and authenticated. • Users are properly authorized before being able to perform sensitive transactions. • Audit and monitoring capabilities are operating.

SECURITY MANAGEMENT (SM) – AUDIT WORK PROGRAM CONTROLS

Please see below for a customized application-level AWP, which contains customized testing procedures based on FISCAM that covers control categories AC, CM, SD, IN and BP:

Configuration Management (CM) Application-Level Controls

Control Technique	Control Description	RoF	Test of Design	Test of Operating Effectiveness
AS-3.1.1 **AS-3.3.1** **AS-3.4.1** **AS-3.5.5** **AS-3.5.7** **AS-3.5.8**	Appropriate policies and procedures are established for application configuration management. Change request forms are used to document requests and related projects. Unit, integration, and system testing are performed and approved in accordance with the test plan, and applying a sufficient range of valid and invalid conditions. Test results are reviewed and documented. Program changes are moved into production only upon documented approval from users and system development management.	Lower	1. Inquire of management and inspect documentation to determine whether a SDLC methodology has been developed that • is sufficiently documented to provide guidance to staff with varying levels of skill and experience, • provides a means of controlling changes in requirements that occur over the system life, and • includes documentation requirements. 2. Inquire with management to determine if • a configuration management process has been developed to control changes to applications, including how changes are requested, authorized, tested (SIT/SAT), and approved prior to being deployed. • change-request forms are used to document requests. • there is a system being used to track change requests such as JIRA or Remedy. 3. Obtain policies and procedures relating to configuration management and determine if they are current and have been approved by management. Additionally, determine if there is a documented process that details how changes are requested, authorized, tested, and approved prior to being deployed to the production environment.	Obtain a population of changes made to the [insert application name] application from [insert testing period]. To confirm the completeness and accuracy of the list, observe the pulling of the list and/or inspect the query used to compile the list. Select a sample of changes and request supporting documentation (change request forms, change approvals, evidence of SIT/SAT testing, and final approval) to determine if changes were appropriately requested, authorized, tested, and approved prior to being deployed to production.

			4. Inspect documentation (e.g., change request, development plans, test plans and results, user acceptance tests, turnover forms and move sheets, management approvals, etc.) related to an example of a recently implemented application change to determine if the actual process reflects the documented process.	
AS-3.6.1	Separate libraries are maintained for program development and maintenance, testing, and production programs.	Lower	1. Inquire with management to determine if separate libraries/environments are maintained for application development, testing, and production. Determine if environments are separated physically or logically, or both. 2. Obtain policies and procedures around how the testing, development, and production environments are separated.	1. Obtain evidence via screenshots, host listing or alternate supporting evidence to determine if the test, development, and production environments are separated.
AS-3.6.2 **AS-3.6.3**	Source code is maintained in a separate library. Access to all programs, including production code, source code, and extra program copies, are protected by access control software and operating system features.	Higher	1. Inquire with management to determine where development source code is stored for the [insert application name] and how access is restricted. Inquire with management to determine who has access to development source code directories, as well as who has access to deploy changes to the production environment. 2. Obtain policies and procedures around how development source code and production environment access is separated.	1. Obtain supporting evidence (i.e. screen shots or directory list) to determine what directories/datasets the source code for the [insert application name] is stored. 2. Obtain supporting evidence via screenshots and other documentation to determine who has access to the development source code directories, what level of access, and if management has approved these individuals to have this access. 3. Obtain supporting evidence via screenshots and other documentation to determine who has access to the production environment directories, what level of access, and if management has approved

					these individuals to have this access.
					4. Compare development source code and production environment user access listings to determine whether developers and users have ability to circumvent controls and update production source code without completing the change request process.
AS-3.14.1	The entity follows an effective process to properly document, test, and approve emergency changes.	Lower	1. Inquire with management to determine if • a configuration management process has been developed with respect to emergency changes to applications including how emergency changes are requested, authorized, tested (SIT/SAT), and approved prior to being deployed; • change request forms are used to document emergency change requests; and • there is a system being used to track emergency change requests such as JIRA or Remedy. 2. Review configuration management policies and procedures to determine if there is a documented process that details how emergency changes are requested, authorized, tested, and approved prior to being deployed to the production environment. 3. Inspect documentation (e.g., change request, development plans, test plans and results, user acceptance tests, turnover forms and move sheets, management approvals, etc.) related to an example of a recently implemented emergency application change to determine		1. Obtain a population of emergency changes made to the [insert application name] application from [insert testing period]. To confirm the completeness and accuracy of the list, observe the pulling of the list and/or inspect the query used to compile the list. 2. Select a sample of emergency changes and request supporting documentation (change request forms, change approvals, evidence of SIT/SAT testing, and final approval) to determine if changes were appropriately requested, authorized, tested, and approved, prior to being deployed to production.

Control Technique	Control Description	RoF	Test of Design	Test of Operating Effectiveness
			if the actual process reflects the documented process. 4. Inquire of management if they have a process to detect if changes have been made to the production [insert application name] without being recorded in the change request system.	

Access Controls (AC) Application Level Controls

Control Technique	Control Description	RoF	Test of Design	Test of Operating Effectiveness
AS-2.3.2 **AS-2.3.4**	The application locks the user's account after a predetermined number of attempts to log on with an invalid password. The application may automatically reset the user account after a specific time period (an hour or a day), or may require an administrator to reset the account. If the user is away from his/her workspace for a preset amount of time, or the user's session is inactive, the application automatically logs off the user's account. Multiple log-ons are controlled and monitored.	Lower	1. Inquire with management and obtain and inspect related policies to gain an understanding of how the system has been configured to prevent multiple log-ons, lock the user account after a predetermined number of log on attempts, and lock a user's session after a predetermined period of inactivity. Inquired with management to gain an understanding of how user accounts are reset after lock. 2. Observe and obtain system configuration screenshots, which show evidence of settings enabled within the application around failed log on attempts, and session locks and determine whether they have been implemented in accordance with policy.	1. Observe an application user attempting to log on multiple times with an invalid password and determine if the user is locked out after a predetermined number of log-ons. 2. Observe an application user attempt to open multiple user sessions and note the result. 3. Observe an application user leave their user session inactive and determine whether the system automatically locks the session after the predetermined allowable period of inactivity.

AS-2.2.1	Identification and authentication is unique to each user. Application boundaries are adequately secure.	Lower	1. Inquire with management to determine how application level users authenticate to the application and if multi-factor authentication is required. Determine if the process is different for privileged application users and non-privileged users. 2. Obtain any policies and procedures around identification and authentication of users and determine if the process is documented.	1. Observe a privileged application user/ application admin and non-privileged application user log into the application to determine if the process is consistent with identified policies and procedures.
AS-2.3.3	Each application user has only one user ID.	Lower	1. Inquire with management and obtain and inspect related policy and procedure documentation to determine whether users are allowed to have more than one user ID and under what circumstances this is allowed and how it is controlled. 2. Inquire of management and inspect relevant policies and procedures to determine if and how the agency handles generic, shared, and system accounts.	1. Obtain a population of [insert application name] application users. To confirm the completeness and accuracy of the list, observe the pulling of the list and/or inspect the query used to compile the list. 2. Determine if any users have duplicate user IDs or more than one user ID. If a user has more than one user ID, obtain supporting evidence to determine whether these instances have been approved based on business need. 3. From the system-generated listing, identify and inspect all generic, shared, and system accounts to understand the business need of each.

AS-2.3.1	The entity has formal procedures and processes for granting users access to the application. The entity's IT security policies and procedures contain guidance for: • assigning passwords; • changing and resetting passwords; and • handling lost or compromised passwords.	Lower	1. Inquire with management and inspect policies and procedures around password parameter requirements and determine if the process and requirements have been documented.	1. Obtain a screenshot of the password settings at the application layer via direct observation. Review security software password parameters and confirm that password-based authenticators • are not displayed when entered; • are changed periodically; • contain alphanumeric and special characters; • are sufficiently long; • have an appropriate life (automatically expire); • are prohibited from reuse for a specified period of time; • enforce a minimum number of changed characters when new passwords are created; • are not the same as the user ID; • contain parameters specific to policies of the organization.
AS-2.4.1 **AS-2.6.2**	Before a user obtains a user account and password for the application, the user's level of access has been authorized by a manager and the application administrator. Owners authorize users to have access to sensitive transactions or activities.	Lower	1. Inquire with management to determine how users obtain access to the [insert name of application] application. Determine if the process is different for application administrator, privileged application user, and non-privileged application user. 2. Obtain policies and procedures for administering access to the [insert name of application] application and determine if they provide guidance for provisioning new user accounts. 3. Obtain and inspect an example authorization of user access performed in the period and determine whether the	1. Obtain a population of application users for the [insert name of application] application. To confirm the completeness and accuracy of the list, observe the pulling of the list and/or inspect the query used to compile the list. 2. Select a random sample of new users (applications security administrators and privileged application users) added since [insert beginning of testing period] based on an approved sampling methodology. Request supporting documentation such as documented

				evidence of new user access forms, approvals, and other supporting evidence to determine if the agency followed its policies and procedures when granting user access and whether the documentation contains • a business need for the user to have access to the account; • a digital or ink signature from the appropriate individual(s); • evidence demonstrating that the user was not granted access to the application prior to authorization; and • evidence demonstrating that the user was not granted unapproved roles.
AS-2.4.2 **AS-2.6.4**	Owners periodically review access to ensure continued appropriateness. Owners periodically review access to sensitive transactions and activities to ensure continued appropriateness.	Lower	1. Inquire with management to determine if there is a process to review access periodically for application administrators, privileged application users, and non-privileged users. Determine the frequency of review. 2. Determine if there are policies and procedures around performing periodic access recertifications. 3. Inquire to determine how management ensures completeness and accuracy of the listing used to performed the periodic access recertification. 4. Obtain and inspect an example review of user access performed in the period and determine whether the review is compliant with policy.	1. Obtain the population of users and select a sample access recertifications performed since [insert testing period]. To confirm the completeness and accuracy of the list, observe the pulling of the list and/or inspect the query used to compile the list. 2. Request supporting evidence of these reviews to determine if the agency followed its policies and procedures when performing the review and whether the documentation contains • a digital or ink signature from the appropriate individual(s); • evidence demonstrating that the agency adhered to the required review frequency; and

AS-2.6.5	Inactive accounts and accounts for terminated individuals are disabled or removed in a timely manner.	Lower		• evidence demonstrating that the agency removed unneeded or inappropriate access in a timely manner.
			1. Inquire with management and obtain and inspect relevant policy and procedure to determine whether there is a process for identifying and disabling inactive and terminated user accounts (application level) in a timely manner.	1. Obtain a population of application users including last log on date, account status (active/inactive) and other critical data elements such as employee ID, user name, roles, etc. To confirm the completeness and accuracy of the list, observe the pulling of the list and/or inspect the query used to compile the list.
			• For inactive accounts, obtain copies of any automated scripts and determine whether it is designed and implemented to identify inactivity based on prescribed thresholds.	2. Filter the listing by last log on date and determine if any users that have passed the inactivity threshold are still active. Follow up with management to determine why these accounts are still active and obtain supporting evidence.
			• For terminated users, gain an understanding of how application administrators receive notification personnel separations and the maximum allowed timeframe to disable these accounts.	3. Obtain a population of separated/terminated personnel to include employees and contractors from [insert testing period] and compare this listing the list of current application users and determine whether user accounts for separated/terminated personnel were disabled/removed in a timely manner. Follow up with management to determine why any active accounts were not disabled/removed.
			2. Obtain and inspect documentation of an example personnel or user separation that occurred during the period.	

| AS-2.8.1 AS-2.9.1 AS-2.10.1 | Policies and procedures are established to reasonably assure that application security audit and monitoring is effective.

Logging and other parameters are appropriately set up to notify of security violations as they occur.

Reportable exceptions and violations are identified and logged. Exception reports are generated and reviewed by security administration. If an exception occurs, specific action is taken based upon the nature of exception. | Higher | 1. Inquire with management to determine

• whether there is a process to log and monitor various security related events within the [insert name of application];

• what security related events are being logged at the application level;

• how long audit logs are retained before being purged;

• what types of monitoring or periodic audit log reviews are being performed;

• how often audit log review occurs;

• who performs audit log review and are they independent of the activities they review (i.e. individual/group does not provision access);

• how the audit log review is documented; and

• how suspicious or unauthorized activity is handled.

2. Inspect policies and procedures around audit logging and monitoring of the [insert name of application] application.

3. Observe and inspect the configuration within the application and capture screenshots to determine if these events are being logged.

4. Obtain and inspect an example audit log review performed during the period. | 1. Obtain and inspect the population of audit log reviews performed from [insert testing period] and select a sample based on an approved sampling methodology. Obtain supporting evidence to determine if log reviews were documented and performed for the sampled dates and any anomalies/ suspicious events/activities were appropriately reported and remediated in a timely manner.

2. Obtain the population of users who perform logged activities. To confirm the completeness and accuracy of the list, observe the pulling of the list and/or inspect the query used to compile the list.

3. Obtain the population of users with access to modify the audit logs. To confirm the completeness and accuracy of the list, observe the pulling of the list, and/ or inspect the query used to compile the list.

4. Compare the population of users who perform logged activities with the population of users with access to modify the audit logs to determine whether audit log integrity is maintained. |

Segregation of Duties (SD) Application Level Controls

Control Technique	Control Description	RoF	Test of Design	Test of Operating Effectiveness
AS-4.1.1 **AS-4.1.2**	Owners have identified incompatible activities and transactions and documented them on a segregation of duty matrix. Owners have appropriately considered risk acceptance when allowing segregation of duty conflicts in user roles.	Higher	1. Inquire with management to determine if management has identified incompatible duties and transactions and documented them in a Segregation of Duties (SoD) Matrix. 2. Obtain a copy of the Segregation of Duties Matrix and any relevant policies and procedures around Segregation of Duties within the [insert name of application].	1. For any identified SoD conflicts, obtain risk acceptance documentation from management to determine if they are aware of the conflicts and have accepted the associated risks. 2. Identify and test any compensating controls to determine if the risk has been sufficiently mitigated.
AS-4.5.1	Process owner has identified the segregation of duty conflicts that can exist and the roles and users with conflicts.	Lower	1. Inquire of management regarding the completeness and accuracy of the report used to identify segregation of duties (SoD) conflicts to include report user listing inputs and report program logic. 2. Inquire of management or observe evidence regarding the last modification date of the SoD conflict report. 3. Obtain and inspect the SoD matrix. Compare the last modification date to the report last modification date and inquire of management regarding any differences.	1. For each relevant data element, randomly select a record from the source system that meets the SoD report criteria and trace the record to the SoD report. 2. For each relevant data element, randomly select a record from the source system that does not meet the SoD report criteria and validate that it does not exist on the SoD report. 3. Select a sample of SoD report reviews and determine whether management performed a review of the reports in accordance with policy.
AS-4.2.1 **AS-4.3.1**	Users are prevented by the application from executing incompatible transactions, as	Lower	1. Inquire with management to determine which types of users can execute transactions within the application. Inquire as to whether application	1. Select a sample of incompatible duties if any are known. Observe an end user or application administrator attempt to

	authorized by the business owners. The profiles for security administrators do not have privileges to input and/or approve transactions.		administrators can execute transactions within the application, and if not, how they are prevented from doing so. 2. Obtain and inspect the SoD Matrix and determine if application administrators are allowed to input, process, or approve transactions within the application. 3. Inquire of management if there are any known instances where SoD cannot be implemented due to resource limitations. If there are instances of SoD, inquire of mitigating controls that management has implemented to mitigate the risk.	perform an incompatible function (i.e. observe the end user attempt to perform an application administrator function and obtain screenshots of error messages. Additionally, observe the application administrator attempt to perform an end user function such as inputting a transaction and obtain screenshots of error messages).

Security Management (SM) Application Level Controls

Control Technique	Control Description	RoF	Test of Design	Test of Operating Effectiveness
AS-1.1.1	A comprehensive application security plan has been developed and documented. Topics covered include: • Application identification and description • Application risk level • Application owner • Person responsible for the security of the application • Application interconnections/ information sharing • A description of all of the controls in place or planned, including how • The controls are implemented or planned to be implemented and special considerations	Lower	1. Inquire with management to gain an understanding as to whether a system security plan has been developed for the [insert application name] application and how often it is reviewed. 2. Obtain and inspect policy over system security plan requirements. 3. Obtain a copy of the latest system security plan and determine if it is current and has been approved by management.	1. Obtain a copy of the latest system security plan for the [insert application name] application and determine if it is compliant with NIST 800-18 or related policy.

	• Approach and procedures regarding security design and upgrade process • Process for developing security roles • General security administration policies, including ongoing security role maintenance and development • Identification of sensitive transactions in each functional module • Identification of high-risk segregation of duty cases • Roles and responsibilities of the security organization supporting the system with consideration to segregation of duties • Security testing procedures • Coordination with entity wide security policies • Procedures for emergency access to the production system, including access to update programs in production, direct updates to the database, and modification of the system change option • System parameter settings, compliant with entity-wide agency policies • Access control procedures regarding the use of system delivered critical user IDs			
AS-1.2.1	Security risks are assessed for the applications and supporting systems on a periodic basis or whenever applications or supporting systems significantly change. The risk assessments and	Lower	1. Inquire with management to gain an understanding as to when the most recent risk assessment has been performed for the [insert application name] application and	1. Obtain a copy of the latest risk assessment or security assessment report performed for the [insert application name] application and determine if it is compliant with NIST 800-30, SP 800-53,

	validation and related management approvals are documented and maintained. The risk assessments are appropriately incorporated into the application security plan.		if it is current, has been approved by management and is supported by testing. 2. Obtain and inspect policy over risk assessment requirements. 3. Obtain a copy of the latest risk assessment and determine if it is current and has been approved by management.	A Rev 4, or related policy.
AS-1.5.2	Security controls related to each major application are tested at least annually.	Lower	1. Inquire with management and obtain and inspect related policy and procedure to determine the scope and frequency of annual security control testing as part of the continuous monitoring program for the [insert application name] application. 2. Inquire with management to determine if security controls are selected and prioritized based on risk.	1. Obtain the results of the most recent annual security control assessment performed to determine if security controls have been appropriately selected and tested.
AS-1.6.1 **AS-1.6.2**	Management has a process in place to correct deficiencies. Management initiates prompt action to correct deficiencies. Action plans and milestones are documented and complete.	Lower	1. Inquire with management gain an understanding as to the process to document, track, and correct deficiencies identified during annual security control assessments, vulnerability scans, and other assessments. Inquire as to what is the allowable timeframe to remediate CAT I, II, and III weaknesses. 2. Obtain any relevant policies and procedures related to the POA&M process.	1. Obtain the latest POA&M for the [insert application name] application and follow up on weaknesses identified to determine if weaknesses are being remediated in a timely manner. 2. Compare the most recent security control Assessment to the current POA&M to determine if weaknesses identified during SCAs are documented in the POA&M and are being mitigated in a timely manner.

| AS-1.7.1 AS-1.7.2 | Policies and procedures concerning activities of third-party providers are developed and include provisions for

• application compliance with entity's security requirements, and

• monitoring of compliance with regulatory requirements.

A process is in place to monitor third-party provider compliance to the entity's regulatory requirements | Lower | 1. As applicable, inquire with management and obtain and inspect relevant policy and procedure to determine how management monitors third-party service providers that support the [insert application name] Application with respect to

• application compliance with DHP's security requirements, and

• monitoring of compliance with regulatory requirements.

2. Obtain and inspect documentation of management's agreement with the third-party service provider to determine whether the arrangement is approved and valid for the period. | 1. Obtain a copy of SOC 1 reports and perform testing based on Kearney template KAT-P-2.9.

2. Perform testing to determine if CUECs are designed and operating effectively.

3. Obtain and inspect evidence of management's monitoring of third-party service providers to include assessment of service provider application compliance with security and regulatory requirements. |

Interfaces (IN) Application Level Controls

Control Technique	Control Description	RoF	Test of Design	Test of Operating Effectiveness
IN-2.1.1	Procedures include a complete list of interfaces to be run, the timing of the interface processing, how it is processed, and how it is reconciled. If system interconnections are used, procedures should address requirements for an Interconnection Security Agreement and Memorandum of Understanding. Timing for processing of the interface has been determined and is followed. A positive acknowledgement scheme is used to ensure that files sent from a source system are received by the target system (i.e., a "handshake" between the systems so that files are not skipped or lost).	Lower	1. Inquire of management and obtain and inspected relevant policy and procedure to determine whether the process for initiating, approving, establishing, and documenting interfaces has been formalized. 2. For each key interface, inquire of management to understand • whether Interconnection Security Agreements, Memorandum of Understanding, or other relevant document have been completed and for each responsible entity and interface; • how interfaced files are processed and reconciled; and • the timing for processing of the interface. 3. For each key interface, obtain and inspect documentation to determine whether they include • a description of the interface; • Interconnection Security Agreement and Memorandum of Understanding; • timing of the interface processing; and • details on how interfaced files are processed and reconciled.	1. Obtain and inspect the Interconnection Security Agreement and Memorandum of Understanding to determine if they are current and were approved by appropriate stakeholders. [Do we know if ISA or MOUs are used within DoD?] 2. Observe interface schedule settings/files to determine whether the interface is configured to execute according to the frequency documented. 3. Observe management generate interface job completion history for the period and determine if jobs were processed at the frequency documented.

IN-2.2.2	The files generated by an application interface (both source and target) are properly secured from unauthorized access and/or modifications.	Lower	1. Inquire with management to determine how files generated by the application interface (both source and target) are properly secured from unauthorized access and/or modification. 2. Observe system settings and configurations and note whether they adequately protect interface files at the source, in transit, and at the target from unauthorized access or modification.	1. Obtain a listing of individuals with access to interface files and inquire of management to determine whether these individuals are approved to have this access.
IN-2.3.1	Reconciliations are performed between source and target applications to ensure that the interface is complete and accurate. Control totals agree between the source and target systems. Reports reconcile data interfaced between the two systems and provide adequate information to reconcile each transaction processed.	Lower	1. Inquire of management to gain an understanding of the process for performing reconciliations between source and target applications and the frequency of review. Additionally, determine if source and target application reconciliations policies and procedures are documented and implemented.	1. Obtain and inspect reconciliation documentation to determine if the data interfaced between the source and target application is complete and accurate.
IN-2.4.1	Management maintains a log for interface processing which accounts for errors and exceptions, as well. Exception/error reports are produced, reviewed, and resolved by management on a regular basis, including correction and resubmission, as appropriate.	Higher	1. Through inquiry of management and review of logs, determine whether errors are properly handled and remediated. 2. Assess the appropriateness of the frequency that exception reports are reviewed (daily, weekly, etc.). 3. Inspect an example exception/error report review performed during the period to determine whether errors were resolved.	1. Select an interface process instance for further inspection. For each relevant data element, randomly select a source system record that meets the interface criteria and trace to the interface file and/or destination system. 2. Select an interface process instance for further inspection. For each relevant data element, randomly select a source system record that does not meet the interface criteria and validate it does not exist within the interface file and/or destination system.

			3. Select a sample of error reports. Inspect documentation of interface error reviews and remediation to determine whether
			• an interface error review was performed in compliance with interface design document timelines, and
			• if interface errors were resolved in compliance with interface design document timelines.

Business Process (BP) Application Level Controls

Control Technique	Control Description	Test of Design	Test of Operating Effectiveness
BP-1.5.1		1. Inquire of management to obtain an understanding of edits used to reasonably assure that input data is accurate, valid, and in the proper format prior to being accepted by the application, including • Authorization or approval codes • Field format controls • Required field controls • Limit and reasonableness controls • Valid combination of related data field values • Range checks • Mathematical accuracy • Master file matching • Duplicate processing controls • Balancing controls 2. Obtain and inspect policies and procedures to determine that appropriate edits are documented, including • Authorization or approval codes • Field format controls	1. Observe an authorized data entry clerk inputting error data in key transaction fields to determine whether they have adequate edit/validation controls over data input. Obtain screen prints of appropriate scenarios and document the result.

		• Required field controls • Limit and reasonableness controls • Valid combination of related data field values • Range checks • Mathematical accuracy • Master file matching • Duplicate processing controls • Balancing controls 3. Inquire of management regarding procedures used to reject and resubmit data for processing, and procedures to provide reasonable assurance that data is not processed multiple times.	
BP-1.5.2		1. Inquire of management to obtain an understanding of overrides and/or bypassing data validation procedures and processes. 2. Obtain and inspect policies and procedure for reviewer override or bypassing data validation procedures. 3. Inspect an override and/or bypassing data validation example and determine whether adequate review and follow up is performed.	1. Obtain a population of override logs that were generated between [insert testing period]. 2. Select a random sample of override logs based on an approved sampling methodology and obtain evidence of proper review/approval of these overrides.

CHAPTER 10
SAMPLING METHODOLOGIES

As you progress into the Test of Effectiveness (TOE) phase of your audit, you will be required to select samples. The concept of a sampling methodology is very simple. Let's say that during the testing of configuration management, we are looking at all the application-level changes made to XXX system since January 1, 2015 to present. Let us say that at this point in the audit, it is now June 30, 2015. June 30 would be the "current" or present point in time. As auditors, we perform our testing at a point in time, thus, we are only focused on changes that occurred in our testing period, which in this case is January 1, 2015 to June 30, 2015.

Now, back to sampling methodologies. Let us say that there were 182 application-level changes for XXX system during our testing period. It would not be feasible to test all 182 changes to determine the operating effectiveness of these controls. Thus, we select a sample and request all the supporting documentation and perform testing on a sample of changes. In doing this, we can then extrapolate our results to the entire population. Another important aspect in sampling is "frequency." The frequency of the control will determine the sample size that should be selected for testing. In this example, we have 182 changes. To determine the frequency, you will use the following chart.

Daily	Weekly	Monthly	Semi Annual	Annual
365	52	12	Twice per year	Once per year

The period of January through June 30 is 6 months. Since we have 182 changes in 6 months, we would multiply 182*2 to get an estimate of how many changes can be expected in a year. We get approximately 364 changes. Thus, we can expect roughly one change per day for this system in scope, making the frequency for this control a "daily control." Now that we have defined the frequency, we will utilize a certain standard to determine the exact sample size. The most common standards are noted below along with the recommended sample sizes and tolerable error rates.

Common federal sampling standards include FAM Sections 360 and 450. Sample item and size selection are based on the auditor's judgment but typically follow guidelines set forth in FAM 450. Items should be selected to produce a sample representation of the population (where all sampling units in the population should have an equal or known probability of being selected) regarding the characteristics being tested. For IT general controls, the sample size selected will correspond with the frequency of control performance as shown in the table below.

Sampling Methodology

Nature of Control	Frequency of Performance	Minimum Sample Size	
		Risk of Failure	
		Lower	Higher
Manual	Many times per day	25	45*
Manual	Daily	15	25

Nature of Control	Frequency of Performance	Minimum Sample Size	
		Risk of Failure	
		Lower	Higher
Manual	Weekly	5	8
Manual	Monthly	3	5
Manual	Quarterly	2	2
Manual	Annually	1	1
Automated	Test one application of each programmed control activity (assumes IT general controls are effective)	1	1

*Per FAM 450.1, a sample of 45 is selected when zero deviations are expected.

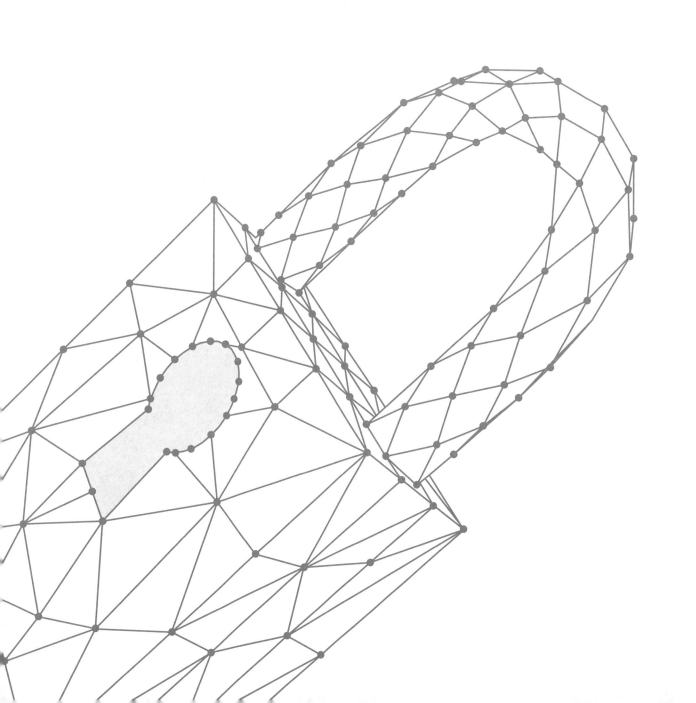

CHAPTER 11

ASSESSING EXTERNAL SERVICE PROVIDERS VIA SOC 1 TYPE-2 REPORTS

• •

As you progress in your IT audit career, you will soon be exposed to the term "SOC Report." There are many different types of SOC reports, and we will discuss them briefly; however, the most important of these reports as it relates to a financial statement audit is a SOC 1 Type-2 report. Let us say we have a federal agency X. This federal agency outsources its data center operations to an external service provider. This external provider is responsible for managing the servers that support this agency and its various systems. Management of the servers may include running vulnerability scans, server baseline configuration scans, patching of the servers, etc. The federal agency in this relationship is known as a "user entity." Depending on how many user entities the external service provider has, they may be required to have an independent assessment of their internal controls performed by an external auditor. The results of this assessment should be in the form of a SOC 1 Type-2 report. Now, when an IPA, or independent public auditor, performs an audit of this federal agency, they will request the SOC report that was performed on the external service provider. The external service provider will provide the SOC 1 Type-2 reports to all user entities on an annual basis so that the user entities can rely on the controls of the external service provider. Another major component of the SOC report is the section on "complimentary user entity controls," or CUECs. CUECs are essentially the portion of a control or an entire control that the user entity is essentially stating that they are not responsible for those controls.

In summary, a SOC 1 Report (Service Organization Controls Report) is a report on controls at a service organization that are relevant to user entities' internal control over financial reporting.

Another example of a service organization that may need a SOC 1 report is a company that provides payroll processing services to user entities. User entities that utilize the services of the payroll processing company may request some independent assurance that their payroll is being processed in a secure manner (i.e. in an environment with sound internal controls). A SOC 1 report provides user entities reasonable assurance that the internal controls of the payroll processing company are designed (Type-1 report) or designed and operating effectively (Type-2 report).

SOC 1 reports can be Type-1 or Type-2 reports:

Type-1 reports are as of a particular date (sometimes referred to as point-in-time reports) that include testing results of the service organization's control design. Type-1 reports test the design of a service organization's controls but not the operating effectiveness.

Type-2 reports cover a period of time (usually 12 months) that include testing results of the service organizations control design and operating effectiveness over a period of time. This is the most effective report that a user entity should be concerned about as it gives the most assurance about the service provider's control environment.

Team K2 has developed our own SOC 1 Testing Template, which is included as part of this book. You can use Microsoft Excel and create three separate tabs. TAB 1 should include your purpose, source, scope, and conclusion.

TAB 2 should contain these columns:

Control Category	Control Activity	Corresponding SOC Report Control #	Control Description	Deviation(s) Noted?	Deviation Details	IMPACT to Audit	IMPACT Justification	Complimentary User Entity Control (CUEC)?	CUEC Description

Populating TAB 2

Step 1: Review the SOC report in its entirety to understand the opinion expressed by the auditor who developed the SOC report. Gain an understanding of the service organizations operations and control environment.

Step 2: Document all the controls tested per the SOC report that pertain to the AC, SD, CM, CP, SM, IN, and BP control categories. Tie these controls into the pre-determined FISCAM control activities defined in the template provided above. Be sure to copy/paste the control descriptions into the template as well (per the SOC report).

Step 3: Document whether there were any deviations relating to these controls tested. Copy and paste the deviations into the template.

Step 4: Determine the impact to user entity based on the deviations noted by assigning a category of High, Medium, or Low. This can become subjective but use your auditor judgment to make the determination. For example, if 30 out of 40 sampled changes did not contain sufficient supporting documentation, the impact to the user entity would be "High" in this instance due to the significance of this deviation on the SOC report. This is an extreme example to illustrate a point.

Step 5: Tie the complimentary User Entity Controls (CUECs) that fall within AC, SD, CM, CP, SM, IN, BP to the FISCAM control activities in the template and populate the template. Copy and paste the CUEC descriptions into the template.

TAB 3 should contain these columns:

Control Category	Control Activity	Complimentary User Entity Control (CUEC) Control Description	Complimentary User Entity Control (CUEC) Testing—TEST OF DESIGN (TOD)	Complimentary User Entity Control (CUEC) Testing—TEST OF EFFECTIVENESS (TOE)	CUEC Effective or Not Effective

Populating TAB 3

Step 1: This TAB is where we document the details of the CUEC testing to determine if these controls are effective. In this TAB, we will map the CUECs to the specific FISCAM control technique in order to document our detailed TOD and TOE steps. Populate this TAB with the CUEC descriptions, applicable control technique, and TOD and TOE steps.

Step 2: We must identify a user entity POC that we can meet with to discuss how the user entity performs the CUEC controls, how they monitor their service provider, and how they manage their CUECs to ensure they are operating effectively. If we cannot obtain a user entity POC that can provide us with this information, we can document the NFR and stop testing. If we can identify a POC at the user entity, we should perform a preliminary meeting to document these details before we proceed with testing.

Step 3: Review any CUEC documentation provided by the user entity relating to a summary of how CUECs are managed and monitored by the user entity. This will help us in tailoring our testing procedures and what documentation to request to perform our testing.

Step 4: Request and obtain supporting evidence and document our testing results to make the final determination of whether controls of the service organization and user entity are appropriate and effective.

CHAPTER 12

AUDIT READINESS 101
(INTERNAL)

• •

When providing "audit readiness services," we are now assisting our client whether it be a federal agency or large commercial entity in ensuring that internal processes and procedures align with the audit standards which apply to it. In this effort, we will assist the federal agency in the PBC process with respect to helping the client identify and respond to PBC requests from the external auditor. We will also assist the client by anticipating what systems may be in scope due to financial impact and other factors. Once we identify "fair game" systems, we need to think like an IPA (Independent Public Auditor) and help the client develop all the necessary internal policies and procedures according to FISCAM, NIST, SOX or any other applicable criteria that can be utilized by the external auditor to identify deficiencies in the client's environment.

THE K2 METHODOLOGY READINESS

The K2 Methodology for audit readiness involves the following:

1. Developing daily/weekly/monthly responsibilities or targets for the audit readiness team:

- Development of "corrective" action plans upon an NFR being issued by the IPA and analysis of milestones to ensure that they accurately address all conditions identified in the NFR and also address the "root cause."

- Checking in with all applicable stakeholders regarding NFR resolution status and providing support as necessary.

- Assisting in the development of certain artifacts, whether it be an SSP, POA&Ms, contingency plan, configuration management plan, access control policies and procedures, SOD matrices, etc.

- Proactively enhancing certain control procedures to prevent future NFRs.

- Proactively identifying future "target" systems to get ahead of the curve and provide support in order to tighten up the control environment prior to the IPA's arrival.

- Conducting an internal audit to help identify control gaps and take countermeasures whether that be the implementation of compensating controls or developing of certain artifacts to mitigate the identified gaps.

The K2 methodology also involves developing two teams:

Red Team:

- Assisting with current active NFR's identified previously and pending artifacts and CAP implementation.

- Assisting with current IPA audit with respect to new artifacts being requested, new NFRs being identified, etc.

- Assisting with weekly meetings with process owners to receive updates on CAP progress.

- Being present during IPA walkthroughs.

Blue Team:

- Assisting client proactively to prevent any future NFR identification.

- Performing internal control assessments on vulnerable high-risk client systems that may or may not have already been selected by IPA for testing.

- Reviewing the results of prior internal audits where gaps have already been identified by the client and areas that we can assist with by proactively working on developing key policies and procedures to address any gaps that could be identified by external auditors in a future audit.

Below is a more detailed/structured process in the support of audit readiness initiatives as it relates to internal controls over financial systems.

INTERNAL CONTROLS OVER FINANCIAL SYSTEMS PROCESS

AUDIT READINESS PROCESS – INTERNAL CONTROLS OVER FINANCIAL SYSTEMS

1.0 Process Cycle

1.1 Task pushed down to audit readiness contractor via government leadership or formal reporting communication medium

The process of executing internal controls over financial systems begins with an inquiry or request from Government Leadership via a formal communication medium. The communication will detail the system that is in scope for review.

1.2   Request to test system (internal audit)

Audit readiness contractor engages its internal IT audit subject matter experts to coordinate with the ICOFS financial team and agree on a parallel plan of action in support of the system in question.

1.3   Initiate communication with system PMO

The audit readiness contractor and IT audit team will then engage the corresponding system PMO via an introduction email that details the purpose and intent of the initial communication. Appropriate background details regarding the financial statement audit and how it impacts the corresponding system PMO is critical in helping them to understand the need for audit readiness contractor support. Additionally, as part of this initial communication, a request for an in-person meeting will be made as well as requesting a listing of all key PMO stakeholders/POCs who should be included in the invite. Logistical details will also be discussed with respect to meeting locations, times based on availability, etc.

1.4   Introduction meeting with system PMO to provide clarity on purpose of audit readiness contractor engagement with PMO.

During the in-person meeting, audit readiness contractor IT audit leads will provide a formal introduction with key system PMO/POCs. The audit readiness contractor IT audit leads will also present an IT audit 101 brief, which will walk the system PMO/POCs/stakeholders through the basics of a financial statement audit including:

- Relevant laws/regulations/methodologies/standards (NIST, RMF, FISMA, FISCAM)
- FISCAM control categories
- Audit process from IT perspective
- Planning
- Testing

- Test of design

- Test of effectiveness

- Reporting

- Examples of controls and testing procedures

- How audit readiness contractor can provide support

Audit readiness contractor will then discuss next steps with the stakeholders and submit an initial Request for Information (RFI), which will help to identify any control gaps with respect to lack of standard operating procedures (SOP's) around critical control processes that the IPA will be focused on testing.

1.5   Participate in meetings with audit readiness contractor IT team

The system PMO stakeholders are requested to participate in and invite all relevant POCs to all audit readiness contractor IT meetings throughout the information gathering and gap analysis process in order for audit readiness contractor team to add value in providing audit readiness support.

1.6   Develop test plan and procedures based on FISCAM and NIST 800-53 Rev. 4

Audit readiness contractor IT team will develop an internal AWP, which details all the relevant FISCAM critical elements, control activities, and control techniques along with testing procedures from a Test of Design perspective. These procedures will mimic a potential IPA audit and will help prepare the system PMO for similar probing questions that would be asked during a formal audit. The audit readiness contractor IT team will develop questions for walkthroughs around access controls, configuration management, segregation of duties, interface controls, and contingency planning, which will correspond to the AWP developed.

1.7   Perform initial risk assessment by conducting walkthroughs of general FISCAM control activities to identify control gaps

The audit readiness contractor IT team will interview the system PMO process owners and perform the walkthroughs according to the AWP developed in the previous step. The audit readiness contractor team will document verbal responses provided by the system PMO and ask relevant questions to address TOD testing procedures from AWP.

1.8   Assist audit readiness contractor in ensuring correct process owners are available during these walkthroughs to add value to process

It is critical that the SYSTEM PMO make sure that all relevant POCs are being included in these meetings so that the audit readiness contractor team is asking the right questions to the right individuals and documenting accurate responses as they relate to the control processes being performed.

1.9   Request applicable RFI items for Test of Design

The audit readiness contractor team will submit a follow up to the initial RFI list which will request various policies and Standard Operating Procedures (SOPs) around various control processes, which are associated with the testing procedures developed and may include follow up requests based on the responses received by the system PMO/POCs during the walkthroughs performed.

1.10   Deliver RFI items

It is critical that the system PMO deliver the requested RFI items in a timely manner. Although this is not a formal audit being performed by an IPA, the level of participation by the system PMO will drive the value that is obtained from this initial gap assessment and will either prevent or cause future NFRs to materialize. Thus, the more support and documentation that is provided by the system PMO to the audit readiness contractor IT team, the more it will help tremendously in preparing the PMO office from the upcoming IPA Audit.

1.11   Identify and document control gaps

After completing the testing based on the AWP performed, the audit readiness contractor team will

- share the results of the assessment with the system PMO via Management Assessment of Results (MARS) and/or Management Corrective Action Plan (MCAP);

- document the results of testing by evaluating walkthrough content and assess policies and procedures against relevant NIST 800-53 Rev. 4 criteria;

- coordinate with the financial team on results to prevent any redundant efforts;

- identify control gaps and areas requiring improvement; and

- develop corrective action plans with detailed milestones and proposed dates of completion to address the deficiencies identified from the internal assessment.

1.12   Assist in internal remediation activities such as development of SOPs

Once procedures noted above have been performed, the audit readiness contractor IT team will hold weekly meetings with the system PMO stakeholders and relevant POCs to begin addressing "internal" CAP remediation milestones prior to IPA engagement to prevent formal NFRs and observations. During these meetings, the audit readiness contractor IT team will cover current CAPs (if applicable), milestones status updates, any items requiring escalation, and any upcoming dates that may impact the system PMO, such as key monthly meetings, etc. Some activities include the following:

- Understanding control process ownership/responsibilities between stakeholders and assisting in Service Level Agreement (SLA) and Memorandum of Understanding

(MOU) documentation to delineate responsibilities to appropriate parties. This will assist in accurate NFR targeting by IPAs so that unreasonable requirements and tasks are not imposed on the system PMO.

- Development of Standard Operating Procedures (SOPs) related to
    - Access controls
    - Configuration management
    - Segregation of duties
    - Contingency planning
    - Interfaces
- Once IPA audit starts, audit readiness contractor will provide guidance on financial statement audit observations, meetings, NFRs, and PBCs.
- Assist with formal communication medium response submissions and coordinate delivery between respective system owners.
- Once IPA audit starts, audit readiness contractor will provide support during IPA site visits and meetings with system PMOs.

1.13 Audit readiness contractor will report assessment results and CAP status

Audit readiness contractor IT team will provide weekly updates to audit readiness contractor and other government leadership as required regarding CAP milestone status and progress in order to drive accountability and progress towards completing CAP milestones and an overall acceptable audit readiness posture.

Internal Use Software Considerations

When assisting as part of the internal audit team, we must also take into consideration any new software being purchased by our client to ensure that IT security is considered prior to purchasing these new software/systems, etc.

Key Considerations of Information Security Controls in the Procurement of Internal Use Software

The decision to procure internal use software (IUS) begins with determining what category of IUS you would like to procure:

1. Commercial Off The Shelf (COTS)
2. Government Off the Shelf (GOTS)
3. Internally developed by government
4. Externally developed by contractor

The reason why these initial decisions are important is that a software that is developed for a specific customized purpose internally by the government or externally by a contractor that is not a COTS or GOTS product must be scrutinized heavily during the SDLC process to ensure that information security has been taken into consideration throughout the lifecycle. COTS and GOTS products, on the other hand, require less involvement as they are usually developed with various security controls built in and can be customized to further lockdown the system or software to an entity's preference.

After the decision has been made in terms of what type of IUS will be procured, the entity must determine if the newly proposed IUS software will be compatible with the current infrastructure and technical environment.

In order to do this, the entity must ask and determine the answers to the following questions in order to make the "Go"/"No Go" decision to procure the software.

CONFIGURATION MANAGEMENT (CM) CONTROLS

1. Has a formal System Development Lifecycle (SDLC) methodology been developed for the newly proposed IUS software?

   A. If NOT, do not proceed with IUS procurement unless an SDLC methodology, which details how security is considered during IUS procurements, is developed.

   B. If Yes, continue to next question.

2. Are security patches regularly available for the newly proposed IUS as vulnerabilities are identified in industry?

   A. If NOT, how will the entity ensure that the IUS is adequately protected from vulnerabilities that are constantly being identified in the industry?

   B. Serious consideration of risk to the entity without implementation of this control by management is highly recommended.

   C. If Yes, continue to next question.

3. Is the newly proposed IUS compatible with the current vulnerability scanner being used?

   A. If NOT, how will the entity identify and remediate vulnerabilities in a timely manner? Unresolved security vulnerabilities can lead to serious data loss and unauthorized access.

   B. Serious consideration of risk to the entity without implementation of this control by management is highly recommended.

   C. If Yes, continue to next question.

4. Are DISA STIGS, CIS benchmarks, or best practice settings available for newly proposed IUS?

A. If NOT, how will the entity ensure that configuration settings of the IUS are secure and customized to the entity's technical environment?

B. Serious consideration of risk to the entity without implementation of this control by management is highly recommended.

C. If Yes, continue to next question.

ACCESS CONTROLS (AC)

1. Can user listings be pulled from the system that include all the roles, groups, and functions associated with those users?

   A. If NOT, how will the entity ensure that user access recertifications are performed periodically?

   B. Serious consideration of risk to the entity without implementation of this control by management is highly recommended.

   C. If Yes, continue to next question.

2. Can password parameters and idle timeout be modified for the newly proposed IUS to align with entity level policy (i.e. length, not displayed when entered, can be changed periodically, user lockout after unsuccessful login attempts?)

   A. If NOT, how will the entity ensure that configuration settings of the IUS are secure and customized to the entity's technical environment?

   B. Serious consideration of risk to the entity without implementation of this control by management is highly recommended.

   C. If Yes, continue to next question.

3. Can audit logs of transactions, admin activities, and other security related events be captured within the newly proposed IUS?

A. If NOT, how will the entity ensure that all transactions and activities performed by administrators are being monitored for unauthorized usage of the IUS?

B. Serious consideration of risk to the entity without implementation of this control by management is highly recommended.

C. If Yes, continue to next question.

BUSINESS PROCESS (BP) AND INTERFACE CONTROLS (IN)

1. Can edit and validation checks be implemented and data overrides controlled in the newly proposed IUS?

   A. If NOT, how will the entity ensure that erroneous data is not being processed through the IUS?

   B. Serious consideration of risk to the entity without implementation of this control by management is highly recommended.

   C. If Yes, continue to next question.

2. Can error reports be generated if erroneous/incompatible data is entered in the newly proposed IUS?

   A. If NOT, how will the entity ensure that erroneous data is not being processed through the IUS?

   B. Serious consideration of risk to the entity without implementation of this control by management is highly recommended.

   C. If Yes, continue to next question.

3. Can the newly proposed IUS interface with key entity systems if necessary?

   A. If NOT, how will the entity ensure that key business transactions and data are being processed between the IUS and key entity systems? **NOTE:** If the IUS does not need to interface with key entity systems, this control is Not Applicable.

B. If Yes, continue to next question.

4. Can master data be protected from unauthorized modification in the newly proposed IUS?

A. If NOT, how will the entity ensure that key data tables that contain vendor information or other important master data are being protected from unauthorized modification?

B. Serious consideration of risk to the entity without implementation of this control by management is highly recommended.

C. If Yes, continue to next question

SEGREGATION OF DUTIES (SOD) CONTROLS

1. Can RBAC be implemented in the newly proposed IUS?

A. If NOT, how will the entity ensure that users of the system are appropriate to have their level of access based on least privilege and job function? How will the entity ensure that privileged users cannot abuse their privileges and perform incompatible functions and transactions without repercussions?

B. Serious consideration of risk to the entity without implementation of this control by management is highly recommended.

After answering the above IUS questionnaire, if you and your client can safely say that the new potential IUS is compliant and/or takes into consideration the above IT security control risks, then it is advisable to proceed with the purchase. However, if not, it is strongly recommended that the new software or system is not introduced, as it will create a plethora of problems in the futures with IPAs that will not be able to be resolved.

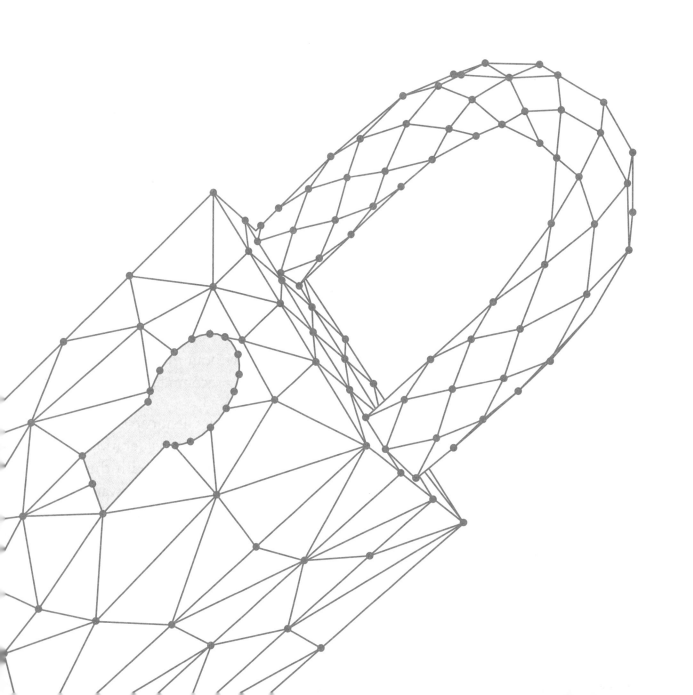

CHAPTER 13

K2 IT Audit Methodologies

IT AUDIT METHODOLOGY

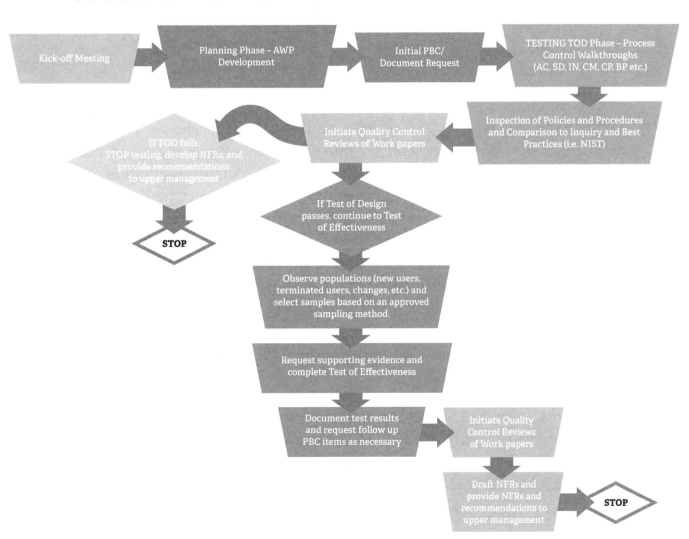

WIN-WIN METHODOLOGY

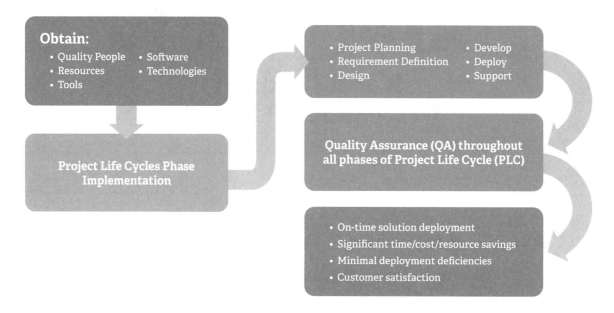

QUALITY CONTROL METHODOLOGY

K2 IT Audit, LLC ensures quality via a multi-step review process. The work products created during an audit include workpapers, supporting evidence, and other relevant documentation. Each deliverable begins as a draft and is prepared by a staff auditor. A senior consultant then reviews it. The senior consultant will distribute comments to the staff auditor to make any necessary corrections or inquire with the client for additional information or clarity to satisfy the objectives of the workpaper or deliverable. Once the comments have been addressed, the senior consultant will perform a final review prior to submitting to the manager. The manager will then perform a review and provide comments as necessary. K2 IT Audit, LLC will ensure a high level of quality in our work products via this multi-level review process.

All work products will have to be reviewed by key management personnel (KMP) prior to being delivered to the end client. K2 KMP have over 30 years of cumulative experience in the field. K2 IT Audit, LLC will hire additional resources at various labor categories and with relevant industry certifications to provide a high level of customer satisfaction and overall quality.

All subcontractors will be subject to the same quality sample NIST Control Standards as employees of K2 IT Audit, LLC. All work performed by subcontractors will be subject to the same multi-level review process and will require final sign off.

In the event a problem is encountered in meeting our deadlines, etc., K2 IT Audit, LLC will provide a timely resolution and action plan, possibly in the form of additional resources, in order to continue providing uninterrupted services to the federal government.

When meeting urgent requirements, K2 IT Audit, LLC will ensure that quality standards are followed in an accelerated manner in order to complete the work on time and within budget, without sacrificing quality of mission critical deliverables.

K2 IT Audit, LLC will have an experienced manager full time at all sites if contracts are being executed at multiple agencies simultaneously. Ibrahim Yussuf will also split time between these sites and projects to ensure quality and check on the status of deliverables and client satisfaction.

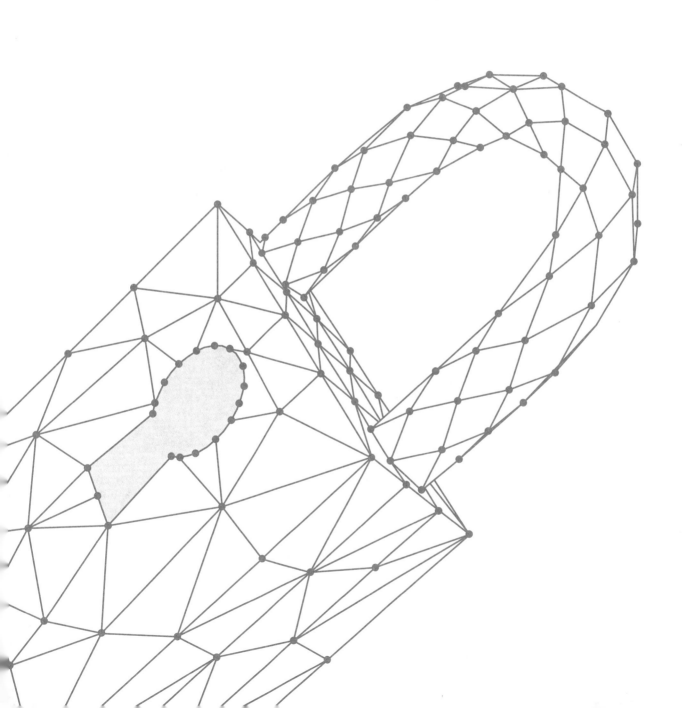

CHAPTER 14

SAMPLE WALKTHROUGH OUTLINE

• •

GENERIC SYSTEM WALKTHROUGH

Does the system have policies and procedures related to the following that have been reviewed and approved within the fiscal year?

1. Access controls: Any policies/procedures/SOPs available?

   - Audit logging and monitoring. What events are logged and who reviews logs?

   - Can audit logs be generated from the system? What types of events are tracked in these logs? Who has access to them?

   - Password parameters. What are the password parameters?

   - User account provisioning and DE provisioning at OS, DB, application layers, and considers transfer, termination, and inactive user disablement.

   - Access recertifications. Frequency?

   - User identification and authentication. How do users authenticate?

   - Can user listings be pulled from the system?

2. Configuration management. Any policies/procedures/SOPs available?

- Is a configuration management plan available?
- How are changes requested, tested, and approved prior to being deployed to production?
- Vulnerability scanning. Frequency of scans? What is the process to remediate?
- Server baseline configurations. Frequency of scans? What is the process to remediate? Tools used?
- Patch management. What is the vendor patch schedule?
- Source code protections?
- Can a population of changes be pulled from the system or are changes tracked in an outside system?

3. Segregation of duties. Any policies/procedures/SOPs available?

- Have incompatible roles been identified and documented in an SOD Matrix?
- Is an SOD policy in place? Is an SOD procedure in place?
- Is management aware of users with conflicting roles and are documented waivers in place to reflect risk acceptance?
- Have sensitive transactions been identified and appropriately segregated?

4. Contingency planning – Any policies/procedures/SOPs available?

- Is a Contingency Plan in place?
- Was a BIA performed as a precursor to the Contingency Plan to identify RPO/RTO information?
- Data backups and restoration procedures?
- Alternate storage sites?

5. Business processes. Any policies/procedures/SOPs available?

   - Edit and validation checks in place?
   - How is access to master data controlled?
   - What are the various inputs and outputs?

6. Interfaces. Any MOUs/ISAs/policies/procedures/SOPs available?

   - Do MOAs or ISAs exist for various system interfaces with XX System that detail what data is interfaced between systems, the interface schedule, error reconciliation processes and procedures, and so on?

7. Incident response. Any policies/procedures/SOPs available?

   - How are incidents identified, categorized, documented?
   - Is there a timeframe for reporting and remediation?

8. Security management

   - Can we obtain a copy of the ATO Package (SSP, POA&Ms, SAR, ATO letter? When is it up for reauthorization?
   - Was a NIST 800-30 based risk assessment performed for the system to identify threats and vulnerabilities?
   - How are annual security control assessments performed?
   - Is there an overall security management plan that talks about risk assessments, annual security control assessments, security awareness training, POA&Ms, system security plan development and maintenance?

After you perform your system walkthrough, you will have to request any PBC items that the client was not able to provide during the walkthroughs. Throughout the walkthroughs you will identify certain documents and supporting evidence needed to complete your testing. Thus, these will need to be requested after you perform your walkthroughs.

1. FOLLOW UP: PBCS TO REQUEST

    1.

    2.

    3.

CHAPTER 15

ASSESSING MATERIALITY DURING A FINANCIAL STATEMENT AUDIT

• •

IT auditors will often find themselves supporting financial auditors during financial statement audits. During these audits, financial auditors will perform testing around financial business processes affecting the general ledger and key financial line items of the agency/system. IT auditors must test the IT controls around these "key" financial systems to provide the financial auditors with assurance that controls are designed and operating effectively. When scoping the IT audit and determining which systems to audit or test, it is imperative that you perform a materiality assessment to determine which IT systems are material from a financial perspective. To do this, you can submit a questionnaire requesting the following information:

1. Volume of transactions processed on an annual basis.
2. Dollar value of transactions processed on an annual basis.
3. Total number of end users that use the application.

These three data elements will provide you with enough information to take back to your financial team and obtain a materiality threshold by which you can then compare against your questionnaire responses and make a determination as to which systems you will be testing. Be sure to set up weekly meetings with financial auditors to make sure you are on the same page with their test plan and that you are providing sufficient coverage to support the financial statement audit.

It is also a good idea to have your financial team review your IT audit work program to ensure that you have sufficient coverage over key controls that they will want to rely on. Additionally, when you perform interface testing and business process testing, you will need to coordinate with your financial team to understand what key interfaces and business processes they care about from a financial perspective so you can tailor your testing accordingly.

CHAPTER 16
CLOSING REMARKS

• •

The field of IT auditing is very exciting and rewarding if you can apply your talents and work to constantly improve your skills and capabilities. Everyone who is starting a career in IT auditing should go take various online trainings and obtain relevant certifications such as the CISA, CISSP, CISM, CRISC, and FITSP-A in order to develop and sharpen their skills in this arena.

We must encourage the younger generation to pursue careers in not only IT auditing but also cyber security and information security, as our nation faces insider threats as well as global threats on a daily basis. New vulnerabilities are exposed daily, and nations such as China and Russia are constantly trying to penetrate our networks in order to exploit vulnerabilities. Although there is no magic pill or solution that can protect us 100 percent, we must do our due diligence to defend against these threats by educating ourselves and becoming subject matter experts within the various domains of cyber and information security. If by reading this book you feel passionate about IT auditing and pursuing a career in this field, we congratulate you for being part of a small group of individuals who have chosen a path that can take you as far as you want to go in life.

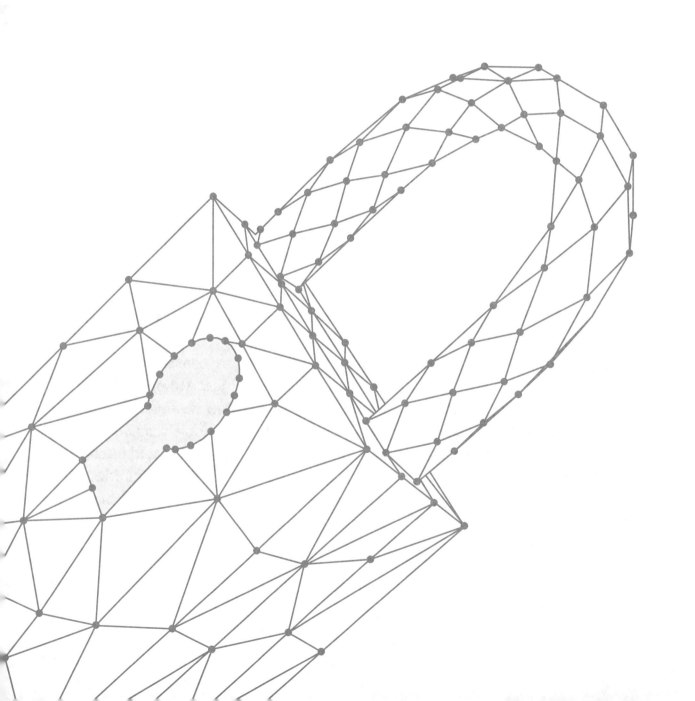

ABOUT THE AUTHORS

IBRAHIM YUSSUF,
President and CEO of K2 IT Audit, LLC

Ibrahim Yussuf has over ten years of experience working within the IT Audit arena at various big four accounting firms. Upon graduating from Virginia Tech in 2008, he worked as an IT Auditor for various consulting firms, including Deloitte and Touche, LLP; Ernst and Young, LLP; and Protiviti. He founded K2 IT Audit, LLC in 2012 and has extensive experience performing controls testing work around IT General Controls and Application Controls at various clients. He is a subject matter expert that has extensive experience performing and teaching.

Presently, Mr. Yussuf operates as the Chief Executive Officer of K2 IT Audit, LLC, a professional services firm that specializes in federal and commercial Information Technology (IT), Audit, and Security services.

MATTHEW ROBINETT

Matthew Robinett, CISSP, CCSP, CISA, COBIT, MSIS, has more than a decade of experience in Audit, Compliance, Risk, and Security. Having been both an auditor and security practitioner, Matthew has spent considerable time advising the business from both sides of the audit relationship. Currently, Matthew oversees risk decision analytics for a large firm within the banking industry, focusing on controls compliance and continuous assurance. Additionally, Matthew is a national conference speaker and has spent more than five years as an adjunct professor teaching a variety of undergraduate and graduate level courses on IT audit and IT security. He holds two undergraduate degrees and a graduate degree from Virginia Commonwealth University. Matthew lives in Richmond, Virginia, with his wife and three children. To this day, Matthew has been unable to effectively explain to his family what he does for a living.